Introduct

If you are reading this, you are almost
enthusiast. You may simply love the th
the ups, the downs, the loops and the
out every possible roller coaster to gai
kiddie coasters. You might be able to rattle off the manufacturer
and design type of almost any coaster you've ever ridden, or have
absolutely no idea how many times you were just inverted on that
last crazy ride. I am somewhere in between.

I began counting the roller coasters that I've ridden as soon as I
realized that other coaster fans kept track of their roller coaster
credits. I am still a novice when compared to many of the really hard
core roller coaster enthusiasts with a mere 208 individual coasters.
And while I love recording my credits, I often can't keep track of
one coaster experience compared with another. After riding 20 or so
roller coasters during a season, the names all seem to run together.
To make things even more confusing, roller coaster names are often
used at several theme parks, but for completely different coasters.
The Joker roller coaster at Six Flags Great Adventure is not the same
coaster as the Joker at Six Flags Fiesta Texas.

I created this journal so that I could keep track of each coaster
immediately after riding it. It helps me to remember the really
wonderful coasters and why I enjoyed them, and the coasters that I
need not ride again because I could hear my teeth rattling the entire
ride. You can even keep track of the differing experiences on the
same coaster depending on where you sit within the coaster train.

I hope that you find this journal/log a handy way to record your
coaster rides and experiences and help you remember specifics about
each one. Enjoy and keep on riding!

Definitions

4th Dimension Coaster: A type of steel roller coaster where riders are rotated independently of the orientation of the track, generally about a horizontal axis that is perpendicular to the track. The cars do not necessarily need to be fixed to an angle.

Accelerator Coaster: A hydraulically launched roller coaster that usually consists of a long, straight launch track, a top hat tower element, and magnetic brakes that smoothly stop the train without making contact.

Bobsled Coaster: A roller coaster that uses a track design that is essentially a "pipe" with the top half removed and has cars that are sent down this pipe in a freewheeling mode. The name derives from the great similarity to the track design used for the winter sport of bobsleigh.

Converted Coaster: Rocky Mountain Construction have converted many former wooden-tracked roller coasters to steel, adding their IBox track to the existing wooden structure.

Dive Coaster: A coaster that features one or more near-vertical drops that are approximately 90 degrees, which provide a moment of free-falling for passengers. The experience is enhanced by unique trains that seat up to ten riders per row, spanning only two or three rows total. Unlike traditional train design, this distinguishing aspect gives all passengers virtually the same experience throughout the course of the ride

Floorless Coaster: A type of steel roller coaster where riders sit with no floor underneath them, allowing their feet to swing freely just above the track.

Definitions

Flying Coaster: A type of roller coaster meant to simulate the sensations of flight by harnessing riders in a prone position during the duration of the ride. The roller coaster cars are suspended below the track, with riders secured such that their backs are parallel to the track.

Hybrid Coaster: A type of roller coaster that has a mixture of wood and steel building materials used for the track and supports.

Hyper Coaster: Any complete circuit roller coaster with a height measuring greater than 200 feet

Inverted Coaster: A roller coaster in which the train runs under the track with the seats directly attached to the wheel carriage. This latter attribute is what sets it apart from the older suspended coaster, which runs under the track, but swings via a pivoting bar attached to the wheel carriage. The coaster type's inverted orientation, where the passengers' legs are exposed, distinguishes it from a traditional roller coaster, where the passengers' arms are instead exposed.

Mine Train Coaster: A steel roller coaster whose trains often depict a set of mine carts, with the forward-most car or portions of it sometimes resembling a small steam locomotive. Most mine train roller coasters are themed in the style of a mine, a Western scene, or simply a mountain range.

Motorbike Coaster: A type of steel roller coaster designed with motorcycle type cars.

Definitions

Pipeline Coaster: A roller coaster where the trains ride between the tracks as opposed to a traditional roller coaster where they ride above them.

Single Rain Coaster: A roller coaster that only rides on one rail instead of the two that other roller coasters ride on.

Side Friction Coaster: An early roller coaster design that has two sets of wheels – normal road wheels and side-friction wheels to prevent the cars from derailing on sharp curves. In comparison, modern roller coasters have a third set of wheels, called up-stop wheels, that allow them to perform steep drops, whereas side-friction coasters almost never featured drops of steeper than 45 degrees.

Spinning Coaster: A roller coaster with cars that rotate on a vertical axis.

Stand Up Coaster: A roller coaster designed to have the passengers stand through the course of the ride.

Steel Coaster: A roller coaster that is defined by having a track made of steel.

Wing Coaster: a type of steel roller coaster where pairs of riders sit on either side of a roller coaster track in which nothing is above or below the riders.

Wood Coaster: A roller coaster that is most often classified as a roller coaster with running rails made of flattened steel strips mounted on laminated wooden track. Occasionally, the support structure may be made out of a steel lattice or truss, but the ride remains classified as a wooden roller coaster due to the track design.

Theme Park:	Date:
Location:	First Ride: Yes No
Coaster Name:	Wait Time:
Park Area:	Ticket Price:
Weather:	Express Pass: Yes No

Crowd:

Coaster Manufacturer:

Coaster Type: Wood   Steel   Hyper   Hybrid   Converted

Coaster Design: (circle all applicable options)

4th Dimension	Accelerator	Bobsled	Dive	Flying	Floorless
Inverted	Mine Train	Motorbike		Pipeline	Side Friction
Single Rail	Sit Down	Spinning	Stand Up	Suspended	Wing

Restraint Type:

Lap Bar   Lap Bar w/seatbelt   Shoulder Harness   Motorbike

Shoulder Harness w/seatbelt   Vest Harness

Other:

Coaster Stats

Height:	Number of Inversions:
Length:	Duration:
Speed:	Cars Per Train:
Drop:	Height Restrictions: min: max:

Other Restrictions: (i.e. lockers required, metal detector, etc.)

My Rating: ☆ ☆ ☆ ☆ ☆   Seat Location: Front   Middle   Back

My Review:

Theme Park: _____   Date: _____

Location: _____   First Ride: Yes   No

Coaster Name: _____   Wait Time: _____

Park Area: _____   Ticket Price: _____

Weather: _____   Express Pass: Yes No

Crowd: _____

Coaster Manufacturer: _____

Coaster Type: Wood   Steel   Hyper   Hybrid   Converted

Coaster Design: (circle all applicable options)

4th Dimension	Accelerator	Bobsled	Dive	Flying	Floorless
Inverted	Mine Train	Motorbike	Pipeline		Side Friction
Single Rail	Sit Down	Spinning	Stand Up	Suspended	Wing

Restraint Type:

Lap Bar   Lap Bar w/seatbelt   Shoulder Harness   Motorbike

Shoulder Harness w/seatbelt   Vest Harness

Other:

Coaster Stats

Height:	Number of Inversions:
Length:	Duration:
Speed:	Cars Per Train:
Drop:	Height Restrictions: min: max:

Other Restrictions: (i.e. lockers required, metal detector, etc.)

My Rating: ☆☆☆☆☆   Seat Location: Front   Middle   Back

My Review:

Theme Park: _____ Date: _____

Location: _____ First Ride: Yes   No

Coaster Name: _____ Wait Time: _____

Park Area: _____ Ticket Price: _____

Weather: _____ Express Pass: Yes   No

Crowd: _____

Coaster Manufacturer: _____

Coaster Type: Wood   Steel   Hyper   Hybrid   Converted

Coaster Design: (circle all applicable options)

4th Dimension	Accelerator	Bobsled	Dive	Flying	Floorless
Inverted	Mine Train	Motorbike	Pipeline		Side Friction
Single Rail	Sit Down	Spinning	Stand Up	Suspended	Wing

Restraint Type:

Lap Bar   Lap Bar w/seatbelt   Shoulder Harness   Motorbike

Shoulder Harness w/seatbelt   Vest Harness

Other:

Coaster Stats

Height:	Number of Inversions:
Length:	Duration:
Speed:	Cars Per Train:
Drop:	Height Restrictions: min: max:

Other Restrictions: (i.e. lockers required, metal detector, etc.)

My Rating: ☆ ☆ ☆ ☆ ☆   Seat Location: Front   Middle   Back

My Review:

7

Theme Park: _____ Date: _____

Location: _____ First Ride: Yes   No

Coaster Name: _____ Wait Time: _____

Park Area: _____ Ticket Price: _____

Weather: _____ Express Pass: Yes   No

Crowd: _____

Coaster Manufacturer: _____

Coaster Type: Wood   Steel   Hyper   Hybrid   Converted

Coaster Design: (circle all applicable options)

4th Dimension	Accelerator	Bobsled	Dive	Flying	Floorless
Inverted	Mine Train	Motorbike		Pipeline	Side Friction
Single Rail	Sit Down	Spinning	Stand Up	Suspended	Wing

Restraint Type:

Lap Bar   Lap Bar w/seatbelt   Shoulder Harness   Motorbike

Shoulder Harness w/seatbelt   Vest Harness

Other: _____

Coaster Stats

Height:	Number of Inversions:
Length:	Duration:
Speed:	Cars Per Train:
Drop:	Height Restrictions: min: max:

Other Restrictions: (i.e. lockers required, metal detector, etc.)

My Rating: ☆ ☆ ☆ ☆ ☆   Seat Location: Front   Middle   Back

My Review:

Theme Park: _____   Date: _____

Location: _____   First Ride: Yes   No

Coaster Name: _____   Wait Time: _____

Park Area: _____   Ticket Price: _____

Weather: _____   Express Pass: Yes   No

Crowd: _____

Coaster Manufacturer: _____

Coaster Type: Wood   Steel   Hyper   Hybrid   Converted

Coaster Design: (circle all applicable options)

4th Dimension	Accelerator	Bobsled	Dive	Flying	Floorless
Inverted	Mine Train	Motorbike	Pipeline		Side Friction
Single Rail	Sit Down	Spinning	Stand Up	Suspended	Wing

Restraint Type:

Lap Bar   Lap Bar w/seatbelt   Shoulder Harness   Motorbike

Shoulder Harness w/seatbelt   Vest Harness

Other: _____

Coaster Stats

Height:	Number of Inversions:
Length:	Duration:
Speed:	Cars Per Train:
Drop:	Height Restrictions: min: max:

Other Restrictions: (i.e. lockers required, metal detector, etc.)

_____

My Rating: ☆☆☆☆☆   Seat Location: Front   Middle   Back

My Review:

_____

Theme Park: _____   Date: _____

Location: _____   First Ride: Yes   No

Coaster Name: _____   Wait Time: _____

Park Area: _____   Ticket Price: _____

Weather: _____   Express Pass: Yes   No

Crowd: _____

Coaster Manufacturer: _____

Coaster Type: Wood   Steel   Hyper   Hybrid   Converted

Coaster Design: (circle all applicable options)

4th Dimension	Accelerator	Bobsled	Dive	Flying	Floorless
Inverted	Mine Train	Motorbike		Pipeline	Side Friction
Single Rail	Sit Down	Spinning	Stand Up	Suspended	Wing

Restraint Type:

Lap Bar	Lap Bar w/seatbelt	Shoulder Harness Motorbike
Shoulder Harness w/seatbelt	Vest Harness	
Other:		

Coaster Stats

Height:	Number of Inversions:
Length:	Duration:
Speed:	Cars Per Train:
Drop:	Height Restrictions: min: max:

Other Restrictions: (i.e. lockers required, metal detector, etc.)

_____

My Rating: ☆ ☆ ☆ ☆ ☆   Seat Location: Front   Middle   Back

My Review:

_____

Theme Park: _____   Date: _____

Location: _____   First Ride: Yes   No

Coaster Name: _____   Wait Time: _____

Park Area: _____   Ticket Price: _____

Weather: _____   Express Pass: Yes No

Crowd: _____

Coaster Manufacturer: _____

Coaster Type: Wood   Steel   Hyper   Hybrid   Converted

Coaster Design: (circle all applicable options)

4th Dimension	Accelerator	Bobsled	Dive	Flying	Floorless
Inverted	Mine Train	Motorbike	Pipeline		Side Friction
Single Rail	Sit Down	Spinning	Stand Up	Suspended	Wing

Restraint Type:

Lap Bar   Lap Bar w/seatbelt   Shoulder Harness   Motorbike

Shoulder Harness w/seatbelt   Vest Harness

Other:

Coaster Stats

Height:	Number of Inversions:
Length:	Duration:
Speed:	Cars Per Train:
Drop:	Height Restrictions: min: max:

Other Restrictions: (i.e. lockers required, metal detector, etc.)

My Rating: ☆ ☆ ☆ ☆ ☆   Seat Location: Front   Middle   Back

My Review:

Theme Park: _____

Date: _____

Location: _____

First Ride: Yes   No

Coaster Name: _____

Wait Time: _____

Park Area: _____

Ticket Price: _____

Weather: _____

Express Pass: Yes   No

Crowd: _____

Coaster Manufacturer: _____

Coaster Type: Wood   Steel   Hyper   Hybrid   Converted

Coaster Design: (circle all applicable options)

4th Dimension	Accelerator	Bobsled	Dive	Flying	Floorless
Inverted	Mine Train	Motorbike	Pipeline		Side Friction
Single Rail	Sit Down	Spinning	Stand Up	Suspended	Wing

Restraint Type:

Lap Bar   Lap Bar w/seatbelt   Shoulder Harness   Motorbike

Shoulder Harness w/seatbelt   Vest Harness

Other: _____

Coaster Stats

Height:	Number of Inversions:
Length:	Duration:
Speed:	Cars Per Train:
Drop:	Height Restrictions: min: max:

Other Restrictions: (i.e. lockers required, metal detector, etc.)

My Rating: ☆ ☆ ☆ ☆ ☆   Seat Location: Front   Middle   Back

My Review:

Theme Park: _____ Date: _____

Location: _____ First Ride: Yes   No

Coaster Name: _____ Wait Time: _____

Park Area: _____ Ticket Price: _____

Weather: _____ Express Pass: Yes   No

Crowd: _____

Coaster Manufacturer: _____

Coaster Type: Wood   Steel   Hyper   Hybrid   Converted

Coaster Design: (circle all applicable options)

4th Dimension	Accelerator	Bobsled	Dive	Flying	Floorless
Inverted	Mine Train	Motorbike	Pipeline		Side Friction
Single Rail	Sit Down	Spinning	Stand Up	Suspended	Wing

Restraint Type:

Lap Bar   Lap Bar w/seatbelt   Shoulder Harness   Motorbike

Shoulder Harness w/seatbelt   Vest Harness

Other:

Coaster Stats

Height:	Number of Inversions:
Length:	Duration:
Speed:	Cars Per Train:
Drop:	Height Restrictions: min: max:

Other Restrictions: (i.e. lockers required, metal detector, etc.)

My Rating: ☆ ☆ ☆ ☆ ☆   Seat Location: Front   Middle   Back

My Review:

Theme Park: _____   Date: _____

Location: _____   First Ride: Yes   No

Coaster Name: _____   Wait Time: _____

Park Area: _____   Ticket Price: _____

Weather: _____   Express Pass: Yes No

Crowd: _____

Coaster Manufacturer: _____

Coaster Type: Wood   Steel   Hyper   Hybrid   Converted

Coaster Design: (circle all applicable options)

4th Dimension	Accelerator	Bobsled	Dive	Flying	Floorless
Inverted	Mine Train	Motorbike	Pipeline		Side Friction
Single Rail	Sit Down	Spinning	Stand Up	Suspended	Wing

Restraint Type:

Lap Bar	Lap Bar w/seatbelt	Shoulder Harness	Motorbike
Shoulder Harness w/seatbelt		Vest Harness	
Other:			

Coaster Stats

Height:	Number of Inversions:
Length:	Duration:
Speed:	Cars Per Train:
Drop:	Height Restrictions: min: max:

Other Restrictions: (i.e. lockers required, metal detector, etc.)

_____

My Rating: ☆ ☆ ☆ ☆ ☆   Seat Location: Front   Middle   Back

My Review:

_____

Theme Park: _____ Date: _____

Location: _____ First Ride: Yes   No

Coaster Name: _____ Wait Time: _____

Park Area: _____ Ticket Price: _____

Weather: _____ Express Pass: Yes   No

Crowd: _____

Coaster Manufacturer: _____

Coaster Type: Wood   Steel   Hyper   Hybrid   Converted

Coaster Design: (circle all applicable options)

4th Dimension	Accelerator	Bobsled	Dive	Flying	Floorless
Inverted	Mine Train	Motorbike	Pipeline		Side Friction
Single Rail	Sit Down	Spinning	Stand Up	Suspended	Wing

Restraint Type:

Lap Bar   Lap Bar w/seatbelt   Shoulder Harness   Motorbike

Shoulder Harness w/seatbelt   Vest Harness

Other: _____

Coaster Stats

Height:	Number of Inversions:
Length:	Duration:
Speed:	Cars Per Train:
Drop:	Height Restrictions: min: max:

Other Restrictions: (i.e. lockers required, metal detector, etc.)

_____

My Rating: ☆ ☆ ☆ ☆ ☆   Seat Location: Front   Middle   Back

My Review:

_____

Theme Park: _____ Date: _____

Location: _____ First Ride: Yes No

Coaster Name: _____ Wait Time: _____

Park Area: _____ Ticket Price: _____

Weather: _____ Express Pass: Yes No

Crowd: _____

Coaster Manufacturer: _____

Coaster Type: Wood   Steel   Hyper   Hybrid   Converted

Coaster Design: (circle all applicable options)

4th Dimension	Accelerator	Bobsled	Dive	Flying	Floorless
Inverted	Mine Train	Motorbike	Pipeline		Side Friction
Single Rail	Sit Down	Spinning	Stand Up	Suspended	Wing

Restraint Type:

Lap Bar   Lap Bar w/seatbelt   Shoulder Harness   Motorbike

Shoulder Harness w/seatbelt   Vest Harness

Other: _____

Coaster Stats

Height:	Number of Inversions:
Length:	Duration:
Speed:	Cars Per Train:
Drop:	Height Restrictions: min: max:

Other Restrictions: (i.e. lockers required, metal detector, etc.)

_____

My Rating: ☆ ☆ ☆ ☆ ☆   Seat Location: Front   Middle   Back

My Review:

_____

Theme Park: _____ Date: _____

Location: _____ First Ride: Yes   No

Coaster Name: _____ Wait Time: _____

Park Area: _____ Ticket Price: _____

Weather: _____ Express Pass: Yes   No

Crowd: _____

Coaster Manufacturer: _____

Coaster Type: Wood   Steel   Hyper   Hybrid   Converted

Coaster Design: (circle all applicable options)

4th Dimension	Accelerator	Bobsled	Dive	Flying	Floorless
Inverted	Mine Train	Motorbike	Pipeline		Side Friction
Single Rail	Sit Down	Spinning	Stand Up	Suspended	Wing

Restraint Type:

Lap Bar	Lap Bar w/seatbelt	Shoulder Harness	Motorbike
Shoulder Harness w/seatbelt		Vest Harness	
Other:			

Coaster Stats

Height:	Number of Inversions:
Length:	Duration:
Speed:	Cars Per Train:
Drop:	Height Restrictions: min: max:

Other Restrictions: (i.e. lockers required, metal detector, etc.)

_____

My Rating: ☆ ☆ ☆ ☆ ☆   Seat Location: Front   Middle   Back

My Review:

_____

Theme Park: _____   Date: _____

Location: _____   First Ride: Yes   No

Coaster Name: _____   Wait Time: _____

Park Area: _____   Ticket Price: _____

Weather: _____   Express Pass: Yes   No

Crowd: _____

Coaster Manufacturer: _____

Coaster Type: Wood   Steel   Hyper   Hybrid   Converted

Coaster Design: (circle all applicable options)

4th Dimension	Accelerator	Bobsled	Dive	Flying	Floorless
Inverted	Mine Train	Motorbike	Pipeline		Side Friction
Single Rail	Sit Down	Spinning	Stand Up	Suspended	Wing

Restraint Type:

Lap Bar   Lap Bar w/seatbelt   Shoulder Harness   Motorbike

Shoulder Harness w/seatbelt   Vest Harness

Other: _____

Coaster Stats

Height:	Number of Inversions:
Length:	Duration:
Speed:	Cars Per Train:
Drop:	Height Restrictions: min: max:

Other Restrictions: (i.e. lockers required, metal detector, etc.)

_____

My Rating: ☆ ☆ ☆ ☆ ☆   Seat Location: Front   Middle   Back

My Review:

_____

Theme Park: _____   Date: _____

Location: _____   First Ride: Yes   No

Coaster Name: _____   Wait Time: _____

Park Area: _____   Ticket Price: _____

Weather: _____   Express Pass: Yes No

Crowd: _____

Coaster Manufacturer: _____

Coaster Type: Wood   Steel   Hyper   Hybrid   Converted

Coaster Design: (circle all applicable options)

4th Dimension	Accelerator	Bobsled	Dive	Flying	Floorless
Inverted	Mine Train	Motorbike	Pipeline		Side Friction
Single Rail	Sit Down	Spinning	Stand Up	Suspended	Wing

Restraint Type:

Lap Bar	Lap Bar w/seatbelt	Shoulder Harness	Motorbike
Shoulder Harness w/seatbelt		Vest Harness	
Other:			

Coaster Stats

Height:	Number of Inversions:
Length:	Duration:
Speed:	Cars Per Train:
Drop:	Height Restrictions: min: max:

Other Restrictions: (i.e. lockers required, metal detector, etc.)

_____

My Rating: ☆ ☆ ☆ ☆ ☆   Seat Location: Front   Middle   Back

My Review:

_____

Theme Park: _____   Date: _____

Location: _____   First Ride: Yes   No

Coaster Name: _____   Wait Time: _____

Park Area: _____   Ticket Price: _____

Weather: _____   Express Pass: Yes   No

Crowd: _____

Coaster Manufacturer: _____

Coaster Type: Wood   Steel   Hyper   Hybrid   Converted

Coaster Design: (circle all applicable options)

4th Dimension	Accelerator	Bobsled	Dive	Flying	Floorless
Inverted	Mine Train	Motorbike	Pipeline		Side Friction
Single Rail	Sit Down	Spinning	Stand Up	Suspended	Wing

Restraint Type:

Lap Bar	Lap Bar w/seatbelt	Shoulder Harness	Motorbike
Shoulder Harness w/seatbelt	Vest Harness		
Other:			

Coaster Stats

Height:	Number of Inversions:
Length:	Duration:
Speed:	Cars Per Train:
Drop:	Height Restrictions: min: max:

Other Restrictions: (i.e. lockers required, metal detector, etc.)

My Rating: ☆ ☆ ☆ ☆ ☆   Seat Location: Front   Middle   Back

My Review:

20

Theme Park: _____ Date: _____

Location: _____ First Ride: Yes   No

Coaster Name: _____ Wait Time: _____

Park Area: _____ Ticket Price: _____

Weather: _____ Express Pass: Yes   No

Crowd: _____

Coaster Manufacturer: _____

Coaster Type: Wood   Steel   Hyper   Hybrid   Converted

Coaster Design: (circle all applicable options)

4th Dimension	Accelerator	Bobsled	Dive	Flying	Floorless
Inverted	Mine Train	Motorbike	Pipeline		Side Friction
Single Rail	Sit Down	Spinning	Stand Up	Suspended	Wing

Restraint Type:

Lap Bar   Lap Bar w/seatbelt   Shoulder Harness   Motorbike

Shoulder Harness w/seatbelt   Vest Harness

Other: _____

Coaster Stats

Height:	Number of Inversions:
Length:	Duration:
Speed:	Cars Per Train:
Drop:	Height Restrictions: min: max:

Other Restrictions: (i.e. lockers required, metal detector, etc.)

My Rating: ☆ ☆ ☆ ☆ ☆   Seat Location: Front   Middle   Back

My Review:

Theme Park: _____ Date: _____

Location: _____ First Ride: Yes   No

Coaster Name: _____ Wait Time: _____

Park Area: _____ Ticket Price: _____

Weather: _____ Express Pass: Yes   No

Crowd: _____

Coaster Manufacturer: _____

Coaster Type: Wood   Steel   Hyper   Hybrid   Converted

Coaster Design: (circle all applicable options)

4th Dimension	Accelerator	Bobsled	Dive	Flying	Floorless
Inverted	Mine Train	Motorbike	Pipeline		Side Friction
Single Rail	Sit Down	Spinning	Stand Up	Suspended	Wing

Restraint Type:

Lap Bar   Lap Bar w/seatbelt   Shoulder Harness   Motorbike

Shoulder Harness w/seatbelt   Vest Harness

Other: _____

Coaster Stats

Height:	Number of Inversions:
Length:	Duration:
Speed:	Cars Per Train:
Drop:	Height Restrictions: min: max:

Other Restrictions: (i.e. lockers required, metal detector, etc.)

My Rating: ☆ ☆ ☆ ☆ ☆   Seat Location: Front   Middle   Back

My Review:

Theme Park: _____ Date: _____

Location: _____ First Ride: Yes   No

Coaster Name: _____ Wait Time: _____

Park Area: _____ Ticket Price: _____

Weather: _____ Express Pass: Yes   No

Crowd: _____

Coaster Manufacturer: _____

Coaster Type: Wood   Steel   Hyper   Hybrid   Converted

Coaster Design: (circle all applicable options)

4th Dimension	Accelerator	Bobsled	Dive	Flying	Floorless
Inverted	Mine Train	Motorbike	Pipeline		Side Friction
Single Rail	Sit Down	Spinning	Stand Up	Suspended	Wing

Restraint Type:

Lap Bar	Lap Bar w/seatbelt	Shoulder Harness	Motorbike
Shoulder Harness w/seatbelt		Vest Harness	
Other:			

Coaster Stats

Height:	Number of Inversions:
Length:	Duration:
Speed:	Cars Per Train:
Drop:	Height Restrictions: min: max:

Other Restrictions: (i.e. lockers required, metal detector, etc.)

My Rating: ☆ ☆ ☆ ☆ ☆   Seat Location: Front   Middle   Back

My Review:

Theme Park: _____   Date: _____

Location: _____   First Ride: Yes   No

Coaster Name: _____   Wait Time: _____

Park Area: _____   Ticket Price: _____

Weather: _____   Express Pass: Yes   No

Crowd: _____

Coaster Manufacturer: _____

Coaster Type: Wood   Steel   Hyper   Hybrid   Converted

Coaster Design: (circle all applicable options)

4th Dimension	Accelerator	Bobsled	Dive	Flying	Floorless
Inverted	Mine Train	Motorbike	Pipeline		Side Friction
Single Rail	Sit Down	Spinning	Stand Up	Suspended	Wing

Restraint Type:

Lap Bar	Lap Bar w/seatbelt	Shoulder Harness	Motorbike
Shoulder Harness w/seatbelt	Vest Harness		
Other:			

Coaster Stats

Height:	Number of Inversions:
Length:	Duration:
Speed:	Cars Per Train:
Drop:	Height Restrictions: min: max:

Other Restrictions: (i.e. lockers required, metal detector, etc.)

My Rating: ☆ ☆ ☆ ☆ ☆   Seat Location: Front   Middle   Back

My Review:

Theme Park: _____ Date: _____

Location: _____ First Ride: Yes   No

Coaster Name: _____ Wait Time: _____

Park Area: _____ Ticket Price: _____

Weather: _____ Express Pass: Yes   No

Crowd: _____

Coaster Manufacturer: _____

Coaster Type: Wood   Steel   Hyper   Hybrid   Converted

Coaster Design: (circle all applicable options)

4th Dimension	Accelerator	Bobsled	Dive	Flying	Floorless
Inverted	Mine Train	Motorbike	Pipeline		Side Friction
Single Rail	Sit Down	Spinning	Stand Up	Suspended	Wing

Restraint Type:

Lap Bar   Lap Bar w/seatbelt   Shoulder Harness   Motorbike

Shoulder Harness w/seatbelt   Vest Harness

Other: _____

Coaster Stats

Height:	Number of Inversions:
Length:	Duration:
Speed:	Cars Per Train:
Drop:	Height Restrictions: min: max:

Other Restrictions: (i.e. lockers required, metal detector, etc.)

My Rating: ☆ ☆ ☆ ☆ ☆   Seat Location: Front   Middle   Back

My Review:

Theme Park: _____ Date: _____

Location: _____ First Ride: Yes   No

Coaster Name: _____ Wait Time: _____

Park Area: _____ Ticket Price: _____

Weather: _____ Express Pass: Yes   No

Crowd: _____

Coaster Manufacturer: _____

Coaster Type: Wood   Steel   Hyper   Hybrid   Converted

Coaster Design: (circle all applicable options)

4th Dimension	Accelerator	Bobsled	Dive	Flying	Floorless
Inverted	Mine Train	Motorbike	Pipeline		Side Friction
Single Rail	Sit Down	Spinning	Stand Up	Suspended	Wing

Restraint Type:

Lap Bar   Lap Bar w/seatbelt   Shoulder Harness   Motorbike

Shoulder Harness w/seatbelt   Vest Harness

Other:

Coaster Stats

Height:	Number of Inversions:
Length:	Duration:
Speed:	Cars Per Train:
Drop:	Height Restrictions: min: max:

Other Restrictions: (i.e. lockers required, metal detector, etc.)

My Rating: ☆ ☆ ☆ ☆ ☆   Seat Location: Front   Middle   Back

My Review:

Theme Park: _____ Date: _____

Location: _____ First Ride: Yes   No

Coaster Name: _____ Wait Time: _____

Park Area: _____ Ticket Price: _____

Weather: _____ Express Pass: Yes No

Crowd: _____

Coaster Manufacturer: _____

Coaster Type: Wood   Steel   Hyper   Hybrid   Converted

Coaster Design: (circle all applicable options)

4th Dimension	Accelerator	Bobsled	Dive	Flying	Floorless
Inverted	Mine Train	Motorbike	Pipeline		Side Friction
Single Rail	Sit Down	Spinning	Stand Up	Suspended	Wing

Restraint Type:

Lap Bar   Lap Bar w/seatbelt   Shoulder Harness   Motorbike

Shoulder Harness w/seatbelt   Vest Harness

Other: _____

Coaster Stats

Height:	Number of Inversions:
Length:	Duration:
Speed:	Cars Per Train:
Drop:	Height Restrictions: min: max:

Other Restrictions: (i.e. lockers required, metal detector, etc.)

My Rating: ☆ ☆ ☆ ☆ ☆   Seat Location: Front   Middle   Back

My Review:

Theme Park: _____   Date: _____

Location: _____   First Ride: Yes   No

Coaster Name: _____   Wait Time: _____

Park Area: _____   Ticket Price: _____

Weather: _____   Express Pass: Yes   No

Crowd: _____

Coaster Manufacturer: _____

Coaster Type: Wood   Steel   Hyper   Hybrid   Converted

Coaster Design: (circle all applicable options)

4th Dimension	Accelerator	Bobsled	Dive	Flying	Floorless
Inverted	Mine Train	Motorbike	Pipeline		Side Friction
Single Rail	Sit Down	Spinning	Stand Up	Suspended	Wing

Restraint Type:

Lap Bar   Lap Bar w/seatbelt   Shoulder Harness   Motorbike
Shoulder Harness w/seatbelt   Vest Harness
Other:

Coaster Stats

Height:	Number of Inversions:
Length:	Duration:
Speed:	Cars Per Train:
Drop:	Height Restrictions: min: max:

Other Restrictions: (i.e. lockers required, metal detector, etc.)

My Rating: ☆ ☆ ☆ ☆ ☆   Seat Location: Front   Middle   Back

My Review:

28

Theme Park: _____ Date: _____

Location: _____ First Ride: Yes   No

Coaster Name: _____ Wait Time: _____

Park Area: _____ Ticket Price: _____

Weather: _____ Express Pass: Yes   No

Crowd: _____

Coaster Manufacturer: _____

Coaster Type: Wood   Steel   Hyper   Hybrid   Converted

Coaster Design: (circle all applicable options)

4th Dimension	Accelerator	Bobsled	Dive	Flying	Floorless
Inverted	Mine Train	Motorbike	Pipeline		Side Friction
Single Rail	Sit Down	Spinning	Stand Up	Suspended	Wing

Restraint Type:

Lap Bar   Lap Bar w/seatbelt   Shoulder Harness   Motorbike

Shoulder Harness w/seatbelt   Vest Harness

Other:

Coaster Stats

Height:	Number of Inversions:
Length:	Duration:
Speed:	Cars Per Train:
Drop:	Height Restrictions: min: max:

Other Restrictions: (i.e. lockers required, metal detector, etc.)

My Rating: ☆ ☆ ☆ ☆ ☆   Seat Location: Front   Middle   Back

My Review:

Theme Park: _____   Date: _____

Location: _____   First Ride: Yes   No

Coaster Name: _____   Wait Time: _____

Park Area: _____   Ticket Price: _____

Weather: _____   Express Pass: Yes No

Crowd: _____

Coaster Manufacturer: _____

Coaster Type: Wood   Steel   Hyper   Hybrid   Converted

Coaster Design: (circle all applicable options)

4th Dimension	Accelerator	Bobsled	Dive	Flying	Floorless
Inverted	Mine Train	Motorbike	Pipeline		Side Friction
Single Rail	Sit Down	Spinning	Stand Up	Suspended	Wing

Restraint Type:

Lap Bar   Lap Bar w/seatbelt   Shoulder Harness   Motorbike

Shoulder Harness w/seatbelt   Vest Harness

Other: _____

Coaster Stats

Height:	Number of Inversions:
Length:	Duration:
Speed:	Cars Per Train:
Drop:	Height Restrictions: min: max:

Other Restrictions: (i.e. lockers required, metal detector, etc.)

My Rating: ☆ ☆ ☆ ☆ ☆   Seat Location: Front   Middle   Back

My Review:

Theme Park: _____ Date: _____

Location: _____ First Ride: Yes   No

Coaster Name: _____ Wait Time: _____

Park Area: _____ Ticket Price: _____

Weather: _____ Express Pass: Yes No

Crowd: _____

Coaster Manufacturer: _____

Coaster Type: Wood   Steel   Hyper   Hybrid   Converted

Coaster Design: (circle all applicable options)

4th Dimension	Accelerator	Bobsled	Dive	Flying	Floorless
Inverted	Mine Train	Motorbike	Pipeline		Side Friction
Single Rail	Sit Down	Spinning	Stand Up	Suspended	Wing

Restraint Type:

Lap Bar   Lap Bar w/seatbelt   Shoulder Harness   Motorbike

Shoulder Harness w/seatbelt   Vest Harness

Other:

Coaster Stats

Height:	Number of Inversions:
Length:	Duration:
Speed:	Cars Per Train:
Drop:	Height Restrictions: min: max:

Other Restrictions: (i.e. lockers required, metal detector, etc.)

My Rating: ☆☆☆☆☆   Seat Location: Front   Middle   Back

My Review:

Theme Park: _____ Date: _____

Location: _____ First Ride: Yes   No

Coaster Name: _____ Wait Time: _____

Park Area: _____ Ticket Price: _____

Weather: _____ Express Pass: Yes   No

Crowd: _____

Coaster Manufacturer: _____

Coaster Type: Wood   Steel   Hyper   Hybrid   Converted

Coaster Design: (circle all applicable options)

4th Dimension	Accelerator	Bobsled	Dive	Flying	Floorless
Inverted	Mine Train	Motorbike	Pipeline		Side Friction
Single Rail	Sit Down	Spinning	Stand Up	Suspended	Wing

Restraint Type:

Lap Bar	Lap Bar w/seatbelt	Shoulder Harness	Motorbike
Shoulder Harness w/seatbelt	Vest Harness	
Other:		

Coaster Stats

Height:	Number of Inversions:
Length:	Duration:
Speed:	Cars Per Train:
Drop:	Height Restrictions: min: max:

Other Restrictions: (i.e. lockers required, metal detector, etc.)

My Rating: ☆ ☆ ☆ ☆ ☆   Seat Location: Front   Middle   Back

My Review:

Theme Park: _____ Date: _____

Location: _____ First Ride: Yes   No

Coaster Name: _____ Wait Time: _____

Park Area: _____ Ticket Price: _____

Weather: _____ Express Pass: Yes   No

Crowd: _____

Coaster Manufacturer: _____

Coaster Type: Wood   Steel   Hyper   Hybrid   Converted

Coaster Design: (circle all applicable options)

4th Dimension	Accelerator	Bobsled	Dive	Flying	Floorless
Inverted	Mine Train	Motorbike	Pipeline		Side Friction
Single Rail	Sit Down	Spinning	Stand Up	Suspended	Wing

Restraint Type:

Lap Bar   Lap Bar w/seatbelt   Shoulder Harness   Motorbike

Shoulder Harness w/seatbelt   Vest Harness

Other: _____

Coaster Stats

Height:	Number of Inversions:
Length:	Duration:
Speed:	Cars Per Train:
Drop:	Height Restrictions: min: max:

Other Restrictions: (i.e. lockers required, metal detector, etc.)

My Rating: ☆ ☆ ☆ ☆ ☆   Seat Location: Front   Middle   Back

My Review:

Theme Park: _____   Date: _____

Location: _____   First Ride: Yes   No

Coaster Name: _____   Wait Time: _____

Park Area: _____   Ticket Price: _____

Weather: _____   Express Pass: Yes   No

Crowd: _____

Coaster Manufacturer: _____

Coaster Type: Wood   Steel   Hyper   Hybrid   Converted

Coaster Design: (circle all applicable options)

4th Dimension	Accelerator	Bobsled	Dive	Flying	Floorless
Inverted	Mine Train	Motorbike		Pipeline	Side Friction
Single Rail	Sit Down	Spinning	Stand Up	Suspended	Wing

Restraint Type:

Lap Bar	Lap Bar w/seatbelt	Shoulder Harness	Motorbike
Shoulder Harness w/seatbelt		Vest Harness	
Other:			

Coaster Stats

Height:	Number of Inversions:
Length:	Duration:
Speed:	Cars Per Train:
Drop:	Height Restrictions: min: max:

Other Restrictions: (i.e. lockers required, metal detector, etc.)

_____

My Rating: ☆ ☆ ☆ ☆ ☆   Seat Location: Front   Middle   Back

My Review:

_____

Theme Park: _____ Date: _____

Location: _____ First Ride: Yes No

Coaster Name: _____ Wait Time: _____

Park Area: _____ Ticket Price: _____

Weather: _____ Express Pass: Yes No

Crowd: _____

Coaster Manufacturer: _____

Coaster Type: Wood   Steel   Hyper   Hybrid   Converted

Coaster Design: (circle all applicable options)

4th Dimension	Accelerator	Bobsled	Dive	Flying	Floorless
Inverted	Mine Train	Motorbike	Pipeline		Side Friction
Single Rail	Sit Down	Spinning	Stand Up	Suspended	Wing

Restraint Type:

Lap Bar   Lap Bar w/seatbelt   Shoulder Harness   Motorbike

Shoulder Harness w/seatbelt   Vest Harness

Other: _____

Coaster Stats

Height:	Number of Inversions:
Length:	Duration:
Speed:	Cars Per Train:
Drop:	Height Restrictions: min: max:

Other Restrictions: (i.e. lockers required, metal detector, etc.)

My Rating: ☆ ☆ ☆ ☆ ☆   Seat Location: Front Middle Back

My Review:

Theme Park: _____ Date: _____

Location: _____ First Ride: Yes   No

Coaster Name: _____ Wait Time: _____

Park Area: _____ Ticket Price: _____

Weather: _____ Express Pass: Yes   No

Crowd: _____

Coaster Manufacturer: _____

Coaster Type: Wood   Steel   Hyper   Hybrid   Converted

Coaster Design: (circle all applicable options)

4th Dimension	Accelerator	Bobsled	Dive	Flying	Floorless
Inverted	Mine Train	Motorbike	Pipeline		Side Friction
Single Rail	Sit Down	Spinning	Stand Up	Suspended	Wing

Restraint Type:

Lap Bar	Lap Bar w/seatbelt	Shoulder Harness	Motorbike
Shoulder Harness w/seatbelt	Vest Harness		
Other:			

Coaster Stats

Height:	Number of Inversions:
Length:	Duration:
Speed:	Cars Per Train:
Drop:	Height Restrictions: min: max:

Other Restrictions: (i.e. lockers required, metal detector, etc.)

My Rating: ☆ ☆ ☆ ☆ ☆   Seat Location: Front   Middle   Back

My Review:

Theme Park: _____   Date: _____

Location: _____   First Ride: Yes   No

Coaster Name: _____   Wait Time: _____

Park Area: _____   Ticket Price: _____

Weather: _____   Express Pass: Yes   No

Crowd: _____

Coaster Manufacturer: _____

Coaster Type: Wood   Steel   Hyper   Hybrid   Converted

Coaster Design: (circle all applicable options)

4th Dimension	Accelerator	Bobsled	Dive	Flying	Floorless
Inverted	Mine Train	Motorbike	Pipeline		Side Friction
Single Rail	Sit Down	Spinning	Stand Up	Suspended	Wing

Restraint Type:

Lap Bar   Lap Bar w/seatbelt   Shoulder Harness   Motorbike

Shoulder Harness w/seatbelt   Vest Harness

Other:

Coaster Stats

Height:	Number of Inversions:
Length:	Duration:
Speed:	Cars Per Train:
Drop:	Height Restrictions: min: max:

Other Restrictions: (i.e. lockers required, metal detector, etc.)

My Rating: ☆ ☆ ☆ ☆ ☆   Seat Location: Front   Middle   Back

My Review:

37

Theme Park: _____   Date: _____

Location: _____   First Ride: Yes   No

Coaster Name: _____   Wait Time: _____

Park Area: _____   Ticket Price: _____

Weather: _____   Express Pass: Yes   No

Crowd: _____

Coaster Manufacturer: _____

Coaster Type: Wood   Steel   Hyper   Hybrid   Converted

Coaster Design: (circle all applicable options)

4th Dimension	Accelerator	Bobsled	Dive	Flying	Floorless
Inverted	Mine Train	Motorbike	Pipeline		Side Friction
Single Rail	Sit Down	Spinning	Stand Up	Suspended	Wing

Restraint Type:

Lap Bar   Lap Bar w/seatbelt   Shoulder Harness   Motorbike

Shoulder Harness w/seatbelt   Vest Harness

Other:

Coaster Stats

Height:	Number of Inversions:
Length:	Duration:
Speed:	Cars Per Train:
Drop:	Height Restrictions: min: max:

Other Restrictions: (i.e. lockers required, metal detector, etc.)

My Rating: ☆ ☆ ☆ ☆ ☆   Seat Location: Front   Middle   Back

My Review:

Theme Park: _____ Date: _____

Location: _____ First Ride: Yes   No

Coaster Name: _____ Wait Time: _____

Park Area: _____ Ticket Price: _____

Weather: _____ Express Pass: Yes   No

Crowd: _____

Coaster Manufacturer: _____

Coaster Type: Wood   Steel   Hyper   Hybrid   Converted

Coaster Design: (circle all applicable options)

4th Dimension	Accelerator	Bobsled	Dive	Flying	Floorless
Inverted	Mine Train	Motorbike	Pipeline		Side Friction
Single Rail	Sit Down	Spinning	Stand Up	Suspended	Wing

Restraint Type:

Lap Bar   Lap Bar w/seatbelt   Shoulder Harness   Motorbike

Shoulder Harness w/seatbelt   Vest Harness

Other:

Coaster Stats

Height:	Number of Inversions:
Length:	Duration:
Speed:	Cars Per Train:
Drop:	Height Restrictions: min: max:

Other Restrictions: (i.e. lockers required, metal detector, etc.)

My Rating: ☆ ☆ ☆ ☆ ☆   Seat Location: Front   Middle   Back

My Review:

Theme Park: _____   Date: _____

Location: _____   First Ride: Yes   No

Coaster Name: _____   Wait Time: _____

Park Area: _____   Ticket Price: _____

Weather: _____   Express Pass: Yes   No

Crowd: _____

Coaster Manufacturer: _____

Coaster Type: Wood   Steel   Hyper   Hybrid   Converted

Coaster Design: (circle all applicable options)

4th Dimension	Accelerator	Bobsled	Dive	Flying	Floorless
Inverted	Mine Train	Motorbike	Pipeline		Side Friction
Single Rail	Sit Down	Spinning	Stand Up	Suspended	Wing

Restraint Type:

Lap Bar   Lap Bar w/seatbelt   Shoulder Harness   Motorbike

Shoulder Harness w/seatbelt   Vest Harness

Other: _____

Coaster Stats

Height:	Number of Inversions:
Length:	Duration:
Speed:	Cars Per Train:
Drop:	Height Restrictions: min: max:

Other Restrictions: (i.e. lockers required, metal detector, etc.)

My Rating: ☆ ☆ ☆ ☆ ☆   Seat Location: Front   Middle   Back

My Review:

Theme Park: _____ Date: _____

Location: _____ First Ride: Yes   No

Coaster Name: _____ Wait Time: _____

Park Area: _____ Ticket Price: _____

Weather: _____ Express Pass: Yes   No

Crowd: _____

Coaster Manufacturer: _____

Coaster Type: Wood   Steel   Hyper   Hybrid   Converted

Coaster Design: (circle all applicable options)

4th Dimension	Accelerator	Bobsled	Dive	Flying	Floorless
Inverted	Mine Train	Motorbike		Pipeline	Side Friction
Single Rail	Sit Down	Spinning	Stand Up	Suspended	Wing

Restraint Type:

Lap Bar   Lap Bar w/seatbelt   Shoulder Harness   Motorbike

Shoulder Harness w/seatbelt   Vest Harness

Other: _____

Coaster Stats

Height:	Number of Inversions:
Length:	Duration:
Speed:	Cars Per Train:
Drop:	Height Restrictions: min: max:

Other Restrictions: (i.e. lockers required, metal detector, etc.)

My Rating: ☆ ☆ ☆ ☆ ☆   Seat Location: Front   Middle   Back

My Review:

Theme Park: _____ Date: _____

Location: _____ First Ride: Yes No

Coaster Name: _____ Wait Time: _____

Park Area: _____ Ticket Price: _____

Weather: _____ Express Pass: Yes No

Crowd: _____

Coaster Manufacturer: _____

Coaster Type: Wood Steel Hyper Hybrid Converted

Coaster Design: (circle all applicable options)

4th Dimension	Accelerator	Bobsled	Dive	Flying	Floorless
Inverted	Mine Train	Motorbike	Pipeline		Side Friction
Single Rail	Sit Down	Spinning	Stand Up	Suspended	Wing

Restraint Type:

Lap Bar Lap Bar w/seatbelt Shoulder Harness Motorbike

Shoulder Harness w/seatbelt Vest Harness

Other: _____

Coaster Stats

Height:	Number of Inversions:
Length:	Duration:
Speed:	Cars Per Train:
Drop:	Height Restrictions: min: max:

Other Restrictions: (i.e. lockers required, metal detector, etc.)

_____

My Rating: ☆ ☆ ☆ ☆ ☆   Seat Location: Front Middle Back

My Review:

_____

42

Theme Park: _____ Date: _____

Location: _____ First Ride: Yes   No

Coaster Name: _____ Wait Time: _____

Park Area: _____ Ticket Price: _____

Weather: _____ Express Pass: Yes   No

Crowd: _____

Coaster Manufacturer: _____

Coaster Type: Wood   Steel   Hyper   Hybrid   Converted

Coaster Design: (circle all applicable options)

4th Dimension	Accelerator	Bobsled	Dive	Flying	Floorless
Inverted	Mine Train	Motorbike	Pipeline		Side Friction
Single Rail	Sit Down	Spinning	Stand Up	Suspended	Wing

Restraint Type:

Lap Bar	Lap Bar w/seatbelt	Shoulder Harness	Motorbike
Shoulder Harness w/seatbelt		Vest Harness	
Other:			

Coaster Stats

Height:	Number of Inversions:
Length:	Duration:
Speed:	Cars Per Train:
Drop:	Height Restrictions: min: max:

Other Restrictions: (i.e. lockers required, metal detector, etc.)

My Rating: ☆ ☆ ☆ ☆ ☆   Seat Location: Front   Middle   Back

My Review:

Theme Park: _____   Date: _____

Location: _____   First Ride: Yes   No

Coaster Name: _____   Wait Time: _____

Park Area: _____   Ticket Price: _____

Weather: _____   Express Pass: Yes   No

Crowd: _____

Coaster Manufacturer: _____

Coaster Type: Wood   Steel   Hyper   Hybrid   Converted

Coaster Design: (circle all applicable options)

4th Dimension	Accelerator	Bobsled	Dive	Flying	Floorless
Inverted	Mine Train	Motorbike		Pipeline	Side Friction
Single Rail	Sit Down	Spinning	Stand Up	Suspended	Wing

Restraint Type:

Lap Bar	Lap Bar w/seatbelt	Shoulder Harness	Motorbike
Shoulder Harness w/seatbelt		Vest Harness	
Other:			

Coaster Stats

Height:	Number of Inversions:
Length:	Duration:
Speed:	Cars Per Train:
Drop:	Height Restrictions: min: max:

Other Restrictions: (i.e. lockers required, metal detector, etc.)

My Rating: ☆☆☆☆☆   Seat Location: Front   Middle   Back

My Review:

Theme Park: _____ Date: _____

Location: _____ First Ride: Yes   No

Coaster Name: _____ Wait Time: _____

Park Area: _____ Ticket Price: _____

Weather: _____ Express Pass: Yes No

Crowd: _____

Coaster Manufacturer: _____

Coaster Type: Wood   Steel   Hyper   Hybrid   Converted

Coaster Design: (circle all applicable options)

4th Dimension	Accelerator	Bobsled	Dive	Flying	Floorless
Inverted	Mine Train	Motorbike	Pipeline		Side Friction
Single Rail	Sit Down	Spinning	Stand Up	Suspended	Wing

Restraint Type:

Lap Bar   Lap Bar w/seatbelt   Shoulder Harness   Motorbike

Shoulder Harness w/seatbelt   Vest Harness

Other:

Coaster Stats

Height:	Number of Inversions:
Length:	Duration:
Speed:	Cars Per Train:
Drop:	Height Restrictions: min: max:

Other Restrictions: (i.e. lockers required, metal detector, etc.)

My Rating: ☆ ☆ ☆ ☆ ☆   Seat Location: Front   Middle   Back

My Review:

Theme Park: _____ Date: _____

Location: _____ First Ride: Yes   No

Coaster Name: _____ Wait Time: _____

Park Area: _____ Ticket Price: _____

Weather: _____ Express Pass: Yes   No

Crowd: _____

Coaster Manufacturer: _____

Coaster Type: Wood   Steel   Hyper   Hybrid   Converted

Coaster Design: (circle all applicable options)

4th Dimension	Accelerator	Bobsled	Dive	Flying	Floorless
Inverted	Mine Train	Motorbike	Pipeline		Side Friction
Single Rail	Sit Down	Spinning	Stand Up	Suspended	Wing

Restraint Type:

Lap Bar   Lap Bar w/seatbelt   Shoulder Harness   Motorbike

Shoulder Harness w/seatbelt   Vest Harness

Other: _____

Coaster Stats

Height:	Number of Inversions:
Length:	Duration:
Speed:	Cars Per Train:
Drop:	Height Restrictions: min: max:

Other Restrictions: (i.e. lockers required, metal detector, etc.)

My Rating: ☆ ☆ ☆ ☆ ☆   Seat Location: Front   Middle   Back

My Review:

Theme Park: _____ Date: _____

Location: _____ First Ride: Yes   No

Coaster Name: _____ Wait Time: _____

Park Area: _____ Ticket Price: _____

Weather: _____ Express Pass: Yes   No

Crowd: _____

Coaster Manufacturer: _____

Coaster Type: Wood   Steel   Hyper   Hybrid   Converted

Coaster Design: (circle all applicable options)

4th Dimension	Accelerator	Bobsled	Dive	Flying	Floorless
Inverted	Mine Train	Motorbike	Pipeline		Side Friction
Single Rail	Sit Down	Spinning	Stand Up	Suspended	Wing

Restraint Type: _____

Lap Bar   Lap Bar w/seatbelt   Shoulder Harness   Motorbike

Shoulder Harness w/seatbelt   Vest Harness

Other: _____

Coaster Stats

Height:	Number of Inversions:
Length:	Duration:
Speed:	Cars Per Train:
Drop:	Height Restrictions: min: max:

Other Restrictions: (i.e. lockers required, metal detector, etc.)

My Rating: ☆ ☆ ☆ ☆ ☆   Seat Location: Front   Middle   Back

My Review:

47

Theme Park: _____   Date: _____

Location: _____   First Ride: Yes   No

Coaster Name: _____   Wait Time: _____

Park Area: _____   Ticket Price: _____

Weather: _____   Express Pass: Yes   No

Crowd: _____

Coaster Manufacturer: _____

Coaster Type: Wood   Steel   Hyper   Hybrid   Converted

Coaster Design: (circle all applicable options)

4th Dimension	Accelerator	Bobsled	Dive	Flying	Floorless
Inverted	Mine Train	Motorbike	Pipeline		Side Friction
Single Rail	Sit Down	Spinning	Stand Up	Suspended	Wing

Restraint Type:

Lap Bar   Lap Bar w/seatbelt   Shoulder Harness   Motorbike

Shoulder Harness w/seatbelt   Vest Harness

Other:

Coaster Stats

Height:	Number of Inversions:
Length:	Duration:
Speed:	Cars Per Train:
Drop:	Height Restrictions: min: max:

Other Restrictions: (i.e. lockers required, metal detector, etc.)

My Rating: ☆ ☆ ☆ ☆ ☆   Seat Location: Front   Middle   Back

My Review:

Theme Park: _____   Date: _____

Location: _____   First Ride: Yes   No

Coaster Name: _____   Wait Time: _____

Park Area: _____   Ticket Price: _____

Weather: _____   Express Pass: Yes   No

Crowd: _____

Coaster Manufacturer: _____

Coaster Type: Wood   Steel   Hyper   Hybrid   Converted

Coaster Design: (circle all applicable options)

4th Dimension	Accelerator	Bobsled	Dive	Flying	Floorless
Inverted	Mine Train	Motorbike	Pipeline		Side Friction
Single Rail	Sit Down	Spinning	Stand Up	Suspended	Wing

Restraint Type:

Lap Bar	Lap Bar w/seatbelt	Shoulder Harness	Motorbike
Shoulder Harness w/seatbelt		Vest Harness	
Other:			

Coaster Stats

Height:	Number of Inversions:
Length:	Duration:
Speed:	Cars Per Train:
Drop:	Height Restrictions: min: max:

Other Restrictions: (i.e. lockers required, metal detector, etc.)

My Rating: ☆☆☆☆☆   Seat Location: Front   Middle   Back

My Review:

Theme Park: _____ Date: _____

Location: _____ First Ride: Yes   No

Coaster Name: _____ Wait Time: _____

Park Area: _____ Ticket Price: _____

Weather: _____ Express Pass: Yes   No

Crowd: _____

Coaster Manufacturer: _____

Coaster Type: Wood   Steel   Hyper   Hybrid   Converted

Coaster Design: (circle all applicable options)

4th Dimension	Accelerator	Bobsled	Dive	Flying	Floorless
Inverted	Mine Train	Motorbike	Pipeline		Side Friction
Single Rail	Sit Down	Spinning	Stand Up	Suspended	Wing

Restraint Type:

Lap Bar	Lap Bar w/seatbelt	Shoulder Harness	Motorbike
Shoulder Harness w/seatbelt	Vest Harness	
Other:		

Coaster Stats

Height:	Number of Inversions:
Length:	Duration:
Speed:	Cars Per Train:
Drop:	Height Restrictions: min: max:

Other Restrictions: (i.e. lockers required, metal detector, etc.)

My Rating: ☆ ☆ ☆ ☆ ☆   Seat Location: Front   Middle   Back

My Review:

Theme Park: _____   Date: _____

Location: _____   First Ride: Yes   No

Coaster Name: _____   Wait Time: _____

Park Area: _____   Ticket Price: _____

Weather: _____   Express Pass: Yes   No

Crowd: _____

Coaster Manufacturer: _____

Coaster Type: Wood   Steel   Hyper   Hybrid   Converted

Coaster Design: (circle all applicable options)

4th Dimension	Accelerator	Bobsled	Dive	Flying	Floorless
Inverted	Mine Train	Motorbike	Pipeline		Side Friction
Single Rail	Sit Down	Spinning	Stand Up	Suspended	Wing

Restraint Type:

Lap Bar	Lap Bar w/seatbelt	Shoulder Harness	Motorbike
Shoulder Harness w/seatbelt		Vest Harness	
Other:			

Coaster Stats

Height:	Number of Inversions:
Length:	Duration:
Speed:	Cars Per Train:
Drop:	Height Restrictions: min: max:

Other Restrictions: (i.e. lockers required, metal detector, etc.)

_____

My Rating: ☆ ☆ ☆ ☆ ☆   Seat Location: Front   Middle   Back

My Review:

_____

Theme Park: _____   Date: _____

Location: _____   First Ride: Yes   No

Coaster Name: _____   Wait Time: _____

Park Area: _____   Ticket Price: _____

Weather: _____   Express Pass: Yes No

Crowd: _____

Coaster Manufacturer: _____

Coaster Type: Wood   Steel   Hyper   Hybrid   Converted

Coaster Design: (circle all applicable options)

4th Dimension	Accelerator	Bobsled	Dive	Flying	Floorless
Inverted	Mine Train	Motorbike	Pipeline		Side Friction
Single Rail	Sit Down	Spinning	Stand Up	Suspended	Wing

Restraint Type:

Lap Bar   Lap Bar w/seatbelt   Shoulder Harness   Motorbike

Shoulder Harness w/seatbelt   Vest Harness

Other: _____

Coaster Stats

Height:	Number of Inversions:
Length:	Duration:
Speed:	Cars Per Train:
Drop:	Height Restrictions: min: max:

Other Restrictions: (i.e. lockers required, metal detector, etc.)

My Rating: ☆☆☆☆☆   Seat Location: Front   Middle   Back

My Review:

Theme Park:	Date:
Location:	First Ride: Yes No
Coaster Name:	Wait Time:
Park Area:	Ticket Price:
Weather:	Express Pass: Yes No
Crowd:	

Coaster Manufacturer:

Coaster Type: Wood   Steel   Hyper   Hybrid   Converted

Coaster Design: (circle all applicable options)

4th Dimension	Accelerator	Bobsled	Dive	Flying	Floorless
Inverted	Mine Train	Motorbike	Pipeline		Side Friction
Single Rail	Sit Down	Spinning	Stand Up	Suspended	Wing

Restraint Type:

Lap Bar   Lap Bar w/seatbelt   Shoulder Harness   Motorbike

Shoulder Harness w/seatbelt   Vest Harness

Other:

Coaster Stats

Height:	Number of Inversions:
Length:	Duration:
Speed:	Cars Per Train:
Drop:	Height Restrictions: min: max:

Other Restrictions: (i.e. lockers required, metal detector, etc.)

My Rating: ☆ ☆ ☆ ☆ ☆   Seat Location: Front   Middle   Back

My Review:

Theme Park: | Date:

Location: | First Ride: Yes   No

Coaster Name: | Wait Time:

Park Area: | Ticket Price:

Weather: | Express Pass: Yes   No

Crowd:

Coaster Manufacturer:

Coaster Type: Wood   Steel   Hyper   Hybrid   Converted

Coaster Design: (circle all applicable options)

| 4th Dimension   Accelerator   Bobsled   Dive   Flying   Floorless |
| Inverted   Mine Train   Motorbike   Pipeline   Side Friction |
| Single Rail   Sit Down   Spinning   Stand Up   Suspended   Wing |

Restraint Type:

| Lap Bar   Lap Bar w/seatbelt   Shoulder Harness   Motorbike |
| Shoulder Harness w/seatbelt   Vest Harness |
| Other: |

Coaster Stats

Height:	Number of Inversions:
Length:	Duration:
Speed:	Cars Per Train:
Drop:	Height Restrictions: min: max:

Other Restrictions: (i.e. lockers required, metal detector, etc.)

My Rating: ☆☆☆☆☆   Seat Location: Front   Middle   Back

My Review:

Theme Park: _____   Date: _____

Location: _____   First Ride: Yes   No

Coaster Name: _____   Wait Time: _____

Park Area: _____   Ticket Price: _____

Weather: _____   Express Pass: Yes   No

Crowd: _____

Coaster Manufacturer: _____

Coaster Type: Wood   Steel   Hyper   Hybrid   Converted

Coaster Design: (circle all applicable options)

4th Dimension	Accelerator	Bobsled	Dive	Flying	Floorless
Inverted	Mine Train	Motorbike	Pipeline		Side Friction
Single Rail	Sit Down	Spinning	Stand Up	Suspended	Wing

Restraint Type:

Lap Bar	Lap Bar w/seatbelt	Shoulder Harness	Motorbike
Shoulder Harness w/seatbelt		Vest Harness	
Other:			

Coaster Stats

Height:	Number of Inversions:
Length:	Duration:
Speed:	Cars Per Train:
Drop:	Height Restrictions: min: max:

Other Restrictions: (i.e. lockers required, metal detector, etc.)

My Rating: ☆ ☆ ☆ ☆ ☆   Seat Location: Front   Middle   Back

My Review:

Theme Park: _____ Date: _____

Location: _____ First Ride: Yes   No

Coaster Name: _____ Wait Time: _____

Park Area: _____ Ticket Price: _____

Weather: _____ Express Pass: Yes   No

Crowd: _____

Coaster Manufacturer: _____

Coaster Type: Wood   Steel   Hyper   Hybrid   Converted

Coaster Design: (circle all applicable options)

4th Dimension	Accelerator	Bobsled	Dive	Flying	Floorless
Inverted	Mine Train	Motorbike		Pipeline	Side Friction
Single Rail	Sit Down	Spinning	Stand Up	Suspended	Wing

Restraint Type:

Lap Bar	Lap Bar w/seatbelt	Shoulder Harness	Motorbike
Shoulder Harness w/seatbelt	Vest Harness	
Other:		

Coaster Stats

Height:	Number of Inversions:
Length:	Duration:
Speed:	Cars Per Train:
Drop:	Height Restrictions: min: max:

Other Restrictions: (i.e. lockers required, metal detector, etc.)

_____

My Rating: ☆ ☆ ☆ ☆ ☆   Seat Location: Front   Middle   Back

My Review:

_____

Theme Park: _____   Date: _____

Location: _____   First Ride: Yes   No

Coaster Name: _____   Wait Time: _____

Park Area: _____   Ticket Price: _____

Weather: _____   Express Pass: Yes   No

Crowd: _____

Coaster Manufacturer: _____

Coaster Type: Wood   Steel   Hyper   Hybrid   Converted

Coaster Design: (circle all applicable options)

4th Dimension	Accelerator	Bobsled	Dive	Flying	Floorless
Inverted	Mine Train	Motorbike	Pipeline		Side Friction
Single Rail	Sit Down	Spinning	Stand Up	Suspended	Wing

Restraint Type:

Lap Bar	Lap Bar w/seatbelt	Shoulder Harness	Motorbike
Shoulder Harness w/seatbelt		Vest Harness	
Other:			

Coaster Stats

Height:	Number of Inversions:
Length:	Duration:
Speed:	Cars Per Train:
Drop:	Height Restrictions: min: max:

Other Restrictions: (i.e. lockers required, metal detector, etc.)

_____

My Rating: ☆ ☆ ☆ ☆ ☆   Seat Location: Front   Middle   Back

My Review:

_____

Theme Park: _____ Date: _____

Location: _____ First Ride: Yes   No

Coaster Name: _____ Wait Time: _____

Park Area: _____ Ticket Price: _____

Weather: _____ Express Pass: Yes   No

Crowd: _____

Coaster Manufacturer: _____

Coaster Type: Wood   Steel   Hyper   Hybrid   Converted

Coaster Design: (circle all applicable options)

4th Dimension	Accelerator	Bobsled	Dive	Flying	Floorless
Inverted	Mine Train	Motorbike		Pipeline	Side Friction
Single Rail	Sit Down	Spinning	Stand Up	Suspended	Wing

Restraint Type:

Lap Bar	Lap Bar w/seatbelt	Shoulder Harness	Motorbike
Shoulder Harness w/seatbelt		Vest Harness	
Other:			

Coaster Stats

Height:	Number of Inversions:
Length:	Duration:
Speed:	Cars Per Train:
Drop:	Height Restrictions: min: max:

Other Restrictions: (i.e. lockers required, metal detector, etc.)

_____

My Rating: ☆ ☆ ☆ ☆ ☆   Seat Location: Front   Middle   Back

My Review:

_____

Theme Park: _____ Date: _____

Location: _____ First Ride: Yes No

Coaster Name: _____ Wait Time: _____

Park Area: _____ Ticket Price: _____

Weather: _____ Express Pass: Yes No

Crowd: _____

Coaster Manufacturer: _____

Coaster Type: Wood   Steel   Hyper   Hybrid   Converted

Coaster Design: (circle all applicable options)

4th Dimension	Accelerator	Bobsled	Dive	Flying	Floorless
Inverted	Mine Train	Motorbike	Pipeline		Side Friction
Single Rail	Sit Down	Spinning	Stand Up	Suspended	Wing

Restraint Type:

Lap Bar   Lap Bar w/seatbelt   Shoulder Harness   Motorbike

Shoulder Harness w/seatbelt   Vest Harness

Other: _____

Coaster Stats

Height:	Number of Inversions:
Length:	Duration:
Speed:	Cars Per Train:
Drop:	Height Restrictions: min: max:

Other Restrictions: (i.e. lockers required, metal detector, etc.)

My Rating: ☆ ☆ ☆ ☆ ☆   Seat Location: Front   Middle   Back

My Review:

Theme Park: _____   Date: _____

Location: _____   First Ride: Yes   No

Coaster Name: _____   Wait Time: _____

Park Area: _____   Ticket Price: _____

Weather: _____   Express Pass: Yes   No

Crowd: _____

Coaster Manufacturer: _____

Coaster Type: Wood   Steel   Hyper   Hybrid   Converted

Coaster Design: (circle all applicable options)

4th Dimension	Accelerator	Bobsled	Dive	Flying	Floorless
Inverted	Mine Train	Motorbike	Pipeline		Side Friction
Single Rail	Sit Down	Spinning	Stand Up	Suspended	Wing

Restraint Type:

Lap Bar   Lap Bar w/seatbelt   Shoulder Harness   Motorbike

Shoulder Harness w/seatbelt   Vest Harness

Other: _____

Coaster Stats

Height:	Number of Inversions:
Length:	Duration:
Speed:	Cars Per Train:
Drop:	Height Restrictions: min: max:

Other Restrictions: (i.e. lockers required, metal detector, etc.)

My Rating: ☆ ☆ ☆ ☆ ☆   Seat Location: Front   Middle   Back

My Review:

Theme Park: _____ Date: _____

Location: _____ First Ride: Yes   No

Coaster Name: _____ Wait Time: _____

Park Area: _____ Ticket Price: _____

Weather: _____ Express Pass: Yes   No

Crowd: _____

Coaster Manufacturer: _____

Coaster Type: Wood   Steel   Hyper   Hybrid   Converted

Coaster Design: (circle all applicable options)

4th Dimension	Accelerator	Bobsled	Dive	Flying	Floorless
Inverted	Mine Train	Motorbike	Pipeline		Side Friction
Single Rail	Sit Down	Spinning	Stand Up	Suspended	Wing

Restraint Type:

Lap Bar	Lap Bar w/seatbelt	Shoulder Harness	Motorbike
Shoulder Harness w/seatbelt		Vest Harness	
Other:			

Coaster Stats

Height:	Number of Inversions:
Length:	Duration:
Speed:	Cars Per Train:
Drop:	Height Restrictions: min: max:

Other Restrictions: (i.e. lockers required, metal detector, etc.)

My Rating: ☆ ☆ ☆ ☆ ☆   Seat Location: Front   Middle   Back

My Review:

Theme Park: _____   Date: _____

Location: _____   First Ride: Yes   No

Coaster Name: _____   Wait Time: _____

Park Area: _____   Ticket Price: _____

Weather: _____   Express Pass: Yes No

Crowd: _____

Coaster Manufacturer: _____

Coaster Type: Wood   Steel   Hyper   Hybrid   Converted

Coaster Design: (circle all applicable options)

4th Dimension	Accelerator	Bobsled	Dive	Flying	Floorless
Inverted	Mine Train	Motorbike	Pipeline		Side Friction
Single Rail	Sit Down	Spinning	Stand Up	Suspended	Wing

Restraint Type:

Lap Bar	Lap Bar w/seatbelt	Shoulder Harness	Motorbike
Shoulder Harness w/seatbelt	Vest Harness		
Other:			

Coaster Stats

Height:	Number of Inversions:
Length:	Duration:
Speed:	Cars Per Train:
Drop:	Height Restrictions: min: max:

Other Restrictions: (i.e. lockers required, metal detector, etc.)

_____

My Rating: ☆ ☆ ☆ ☆ ☆   Seat Location: Front   Middle   Back

My Review:

_____

Theme Park:	Date:
Location:	First Ride: Yes No
Coaster Name:	Wait Time:
Park Area:	Ticket Price:
Weather:	Express Pass: Yes No

Crowd:

Coaster Manufacturer:

Coaster Type: Wood   Steel   Hyper   Hybrid   Converted

Coaster Design: (circle all applicable options)

4th Dimension	Accelerator	Bobsled	Dive	Flying	Floorless
Inverted	Mine Train	Motorbike	Pipeline		Side Friction
Single Rail	Sit Down	Spinning	Stand Up	Suspended	Wing

Restraint Type:

Lap Bar   Lap Bar w/seatbelt   Shoulder Harness   Motorbike

Shoulder Harness w/seatbelt   Vest Harness

Other:

Coaster Stats

Height:	Number of Inversions:
Length:	Duration:
Speed:	Cars Per Train:
Drop:	Height Restrictions: min: max:

Other Restrictions: (i.e. lockers required, metal detector, etc.)

My Rating: ☆☆☆☆☆   Seat Location: Front   Middle   Back

My Review:

Theme Park: _____   Date: _____

Location: _____   First Ride: Yes   No

Coaster Name: _____   Wait Time: _____

Park Area: _____   Ticket Price: _____

Weather: _____   Express Pass: Yes   No

Crowd: _____

Coaster Manufacturer: _____

Coaster Type: Wood   Steel   Hyper   Hybrid   Converted

Coaster Design: (circle all applicable options)

4th Dimension	Accelerator	Bobsled	Dive	Flying	Floorless
Inverted	Mine Train	Motorbike		Pipeline	Side Friction
Single Rail	Sit Down	Spinning	Stand Up	Suspended	Wing

Restraint Type:

Lap Bar	Lap Bar w/seatbelt	Shoulder Harness	Motorbike
Shoulder Harness w/seatbelt		Vest Harness	
Other:			

Coaster Stats

Height:	Number of Inversions:
Length:	Duration:
Speed:	Cars Per Train:
Drop:	Height Restrictions: min: max:

Other Restrictions: (i.e. lockers required, metal detector, etc.)

My Rating: ☆ ☆ ☆ ☆ ☆   Seat Location: Front   Middle   Back

My Review:

Theme Park: _____ Date: _____

Location: _____ First Ride: Yes   No

Coaster Name: _____ Wait Time: _____

Park Area: _____ Ticket Price: _____

Weather: _____ Express Pass: Yes   No

Crowd: _____

Coaster Manufacturer: _____

Coaster Type: Wood   Steel   Hyper   Hybrid   Converted

Coaster Design: (circle all applicable options)

4th Dimension	Accelerator	Bobsled	Dive	Flying	Floorless
Inverted	Mine Train	Motorbike	Pipeline		Side Friction
Single Rail	Sit Down	Spinning	Stand Up	Suspended	Wing

Restraint Type:

Lap Bar   Lap Bar w/seatbelt   Shoulder Harness   Motorbike

Shoulder Harness w/seatbelt   Vest Harness

Other:

Coaster Stats

Height:	Number of Inversions:
Length:	Duration:
Speed:	Cars Per Train:
Drop:	Height Restrictions: min: max:

Other Restrictions: (i.e. lockers required, metal detector, etc.)

My Rating: ☆ ☆ ☆ ☆ ☆   Seat Location: Front   Middle   Back

My Review:

Theme Park: _____ Date: _____

Location: _____ First Ride: Yes No

Coaster Name: _____ Wait Time: _____

Park Area: _____ Ticket Price: _____

Weather: _____ Express Pass: Yes No

Crowd: _____

Coaster Manufacturer: _____

Coaster Type: Wood   Steel   Hyper   Hybrid   Converted

Coaster Design: (circle all applicable options)

4th Dimension	Accelerator	Bobsled	Dive	Flying	Floorless
Inverted	Mine Train	Motorbike	Pipeline		Side Friction
Single Rail	Sit Down	Spinning	Stand Up	Suspended	Wing

Restraint Type:

Lap Bar   Lap Bar w/seatbelt   Shoulder Harness   Motorbike

Shoulder Harness w/seatbelt   Vest Harness

Other: _____

Coaster Stats

Height:	Number of Inversions:
Length:	Duration:
Speed:	Cars Per Train:
Drop:	Height Restrictions: min: max:

Other Restrictions: (i.e. lockers required, metal detector, etc.)

My Rating: ☆ ☆ ☆ ☆ ☆   Seat Location: Front   Middle   Back

My Review:

Theme Park: _____ Date: _____

Location: _____ First Ride: Yes   No

Coaster Name: _____ Wait Time: _____

Park Area: _____ Ticket Price: _____

Weather: _____ Express Pass: Yes   No

Crowd: _____

Coaster Manufacturer: _____

Coaster Type: Wood   Steel   Hyper   Hybrid   Converted

Coaster Design: (circle all applicable options)

4th Dimension	Accelerator	Bobsled	Dive	Flying	Floorless
Inverted	Mine Train	Motorbike	Pipeline		Side Friction
Single Rail	Sit Down	Spinning	Stand Up	Suspended	Wing

Restraint Type:

Lap Bar	Lap Bar w/seatbelt	Shoulder Harness	Motorbike
Shoulder Harness w/seatbelt		Vest Harness	
Other:			

Coaster Stats

Height:	Number of Inversions:
Length:	Duration:
Speed:	Cars Per Train:
Drop:	Height Restrictions: min: max:

Other Restrictions: (i.e. lockers required, metal detector, etc.)

_____

My Rating: ☆ ☆ ☆ ☆ ☆   Seat Location: Front   Middle   Back

My Review:

_____

Theme Park: _____ Date: _____

Location: _____ First Ride: Yes   No

Coaster Name: _____ Wait Time: _____

Park Area: _____ Ticket Price: _____

Weather: _____ Express Pass: Yes   No

Crowd: _____

Coaster Manufacturer: _____

Coaster Type: Wood   Steel   Hyper   Hybrid   Converted

Coaster Design: (circle all applicable options)

4th Dimension	Accelerator	Bobsled	Dive	Flying	Floorless
Inverted	Mine Train	Motorbike	Pipeline		Side Friction
Single Rail	Sit Down	Spinning	Stand Up	Suspended	Wing

Restraint Type:

Lap Bar   Lap Bar w/seatbelt   Shoulder Harness   Motorbike

Shoulder Harness w/seatbelt   Vest Harness

Other: _____

Coaster Stats

Height:	Number of Inversions:
Length:	Duration:
Speed:	Cars Per Train:
Drop:	Height Restrictions: min: max:

Other Restrictions: (i.e. lockers required, metal detector, etc.)

My Rating: ☆ ☆ ☆ ☆ ☆   Seat Location: Front   Middle   Back

My Review:

Theme Park: _____ | Date: _____

Location: _____ | First Ride: Yes   No

Coaster Name: _____ | Wait Time: _____

Park Area: _____ | Ticket Price: _____

Weather: _____ | Express Pass: Yes No

Crowd: _____

Coaster Manufacturer: _____

Coaster Type: Wood   Steel   Hyper   Hybrid   Converted

Coaster Design: (circle all applicable options)

4th Dimension	Accelerator	Bobsled	Dive	Flying	Floorless
Inverted	Mine Train	Motorbike	Pipeline		Side Friction
Single Rail	Sit Down	Spinning	Stand Up	Suspended	Wing

Restraint Type:

Lap Bar   Lap Bar w/seatbelt   Shoulder Harness   Motorbike

Shoulder Harness w/seatbelt   Vest Harness

Other:

Coaster Stats

Height:	Number of Inversions:
Length:	Duration:
Speed:	Cars Per Train:
Drop:	Height Restrictions: min: max:

Other Restrictions: (i.e. lockers required, metal detector, etc.)

My Rating: ☆☆☆☆☆   Seat Location: Front   Middle   Back

My Review:

Theme Park: _____ Date: _____

Location: _____ First Ride: Yes   No

Coaster Name: _____ Wait Time: _____

Park Area: _____ Ticket Price: _____

Weather: _____ Express Pass: Yes   No

Crowd: _____

Coaster Manufacturer: _____

Coaster Type: Wood   Steel   Hyper   Hybrid   Converted

Coaster Design: (circle all applicable options)

4th Dimension	Accelerator	Bobsled	Dive	Flying	Floorless
Inverted	Mine Train	Motorbike		Pipeline	Side Friction
Single Rail	Sit Down	Spinning	Stand Up	Suspended	Wing

Restraint Type:

Lap Bar   Lap Bar w/seatbelt   Shoulder Harness   Motorbike

Shoulder Harness w/seatbelt   Vest Harness

Other: _____

Coaster Stats

Height:	Number of Inversions:
Length:	Duration:
Speed:	Cars Per Train:
Drop:	Height Restrictions: min: max:

Other Restrictions: (i.e. lockers required, metal detector, etc.)

My Rating: ☆ ☆ ☆ ☆ ☆   Seat Location: Front   Middle   Back

My Review:

70

Theme Park: _____   Date: _____

Location: _____   First Ride: Yes   No

Coaster Name: _____   Wait Time: _____

Park Area: _____   Ticket Price: _____

Weather: _____   Express Pass: Yes   No

Crowd: _____

Coaster Manufacturer: _____

Coaster Type: Wood   Steel   Hyper   Hybrid   Converted

Coaster Design: (circle all applicable options)

4th Dimension	Accelerator	Bobsled	Dive	Flying	Floorless
Inverted	Mine Train	Motorbike	Pipeline		Side Friction
Single Rail	Sit Down	Spinning	Stand Up	Suspended	Wing

Restraint Type:

Lap Bar   Lap Bar w/seatbelt   Shoulder Harness   Motorbike

Shoulder Harness w/seatbelt   Vest Harness

Other: _____

Coaster Stats

Height:	Number of Inversions:
Length:	Duration:
Speed:	Cars Per Train:
Drop:	Height Restrictions: min: max:

Other Restrictions: (i.e. lockers required, metal detector, etc.)

My Rating: ☆ ☆ ☆ ☆ ☆   Seat Location: Front   Middle   Back

My Review:

Theme Park: _____   Date: _____

Location: _____   First Ride: Yes   No

Coaster Name: _____   Wait Time: _____

Park Area: _____   Ticket Price: _____

Weather: _____   Express Pass: Yes   No

Crowd: _____

Coaster Manufacturer: _____

Coaster Type: Wood   Steel   Hyper   Hybrid   Converted

Coaster Design: (circle all applicable options)

4th Dimension	Accelerator	Bobsled	Dive	Flying	Floorless
Inverted	Mine Train	Motorbike	Pipeline		Side Friction
Single Rail	Sit Down	Spinning	Stand Up	Suspended	Wing

Restraint Type:

Lap Bar   Lap Bar w/seatbelt   Shoulder Harness   Motorbike

Shoulder Harness w/seatbelt   Vest Harness

Other: _____

Coaster Stats

Height:	Number of Inversions:
Length:	Duration:
Speed:	Cars Per Train:
Drop:	Height Restrictions: min: max:

Other Restrictions: (i.e. lockers required, metal detector, etc.)

My Rating: ☆ ☆ ☆ ☆ ☆   Seat Location: Front   Middle   Back

My Review:

Theme Park: _____ Date: _____

Location: _____ First Ride: Yes   No

Coaster Name: _____ Wait Time: _____

Park Area: _____ Ticket Price: _____

Weather: _____ Express Pass: Yes No

Crowd: _____

Coaster Manufacturer: _____

Coaster Type: Wood   Steel   Hyper   Hybrid   Converted

Coaster Design: (circle all applicable options)

4th Dimension	Accelerator	Bobsled	Dive	Flying	Floorless
Inverted	Mine Train	Motorbike	Pipeline		Side Friction
Single Rail	Sit Down	Spinning	Stand Up	Suspended	Wing

Restraint Type:

Lap Bar   Lap Bar w/seatbelt   Shoulder Harness   Motorbike

Shoulder Harness w/seatbelt   Vest Harness

Other: _____

Coaster Stats

Height:	Number of Inversions:
Length:	Duration:
Speed:	Cars Per Train:
Drop:	Height Restrictions: min: max:

Other Restrictions: (i.e. lockers required, metal detector, etc.)

My Rating: ☆ ☆ ☆ ☆ ☆   Seat Location: Front   Middle   Back

My Review:

73

Theme Park: _____   Date: _____

Location: _____   First Ride: Yes   No

Coaster Name: _____   Wait Time: _____

Park Area: _____   Ticket Price: _____

Weather: _____   Express Pass: Yes   No

Crowd: _____

Coaster Manufacturer: _____

Coaster Type: Wood   Steel   Hyper   Hybrid   Converted

Coaster Design: (circle all applicable options)

4th Dimension	Accelerator	Bobsled	Dive	Flying	Floorless
Inverted	Mine Train	Motorbike	Pipeline		Side Friction
Single Rail	Sit Down	Spinning	Stand Up	Suspended	Wing

Restraint Type:

Lap Bar   Lap Bar w/seatbelt   Shoulder Harness   Motorbike

Shoulder Harness w/seatbelt   Vest Harness

Other: _____

Coaster Stats

Height:	Number of Inversions:
Length:	Duration:
Speed:	Cars Per Train:
Drop:	Height Restrictions: min: max:

Other Restrictions: (i.e. lockers required, metal detector, etc.)

My Rating: ☆ ☆ ☆ ☆ ☆   Seat Location: Front   Middle   Back

My Review:

Theme Park: _____   Date: _____

Location: _____   First Ride: Yes   No

Coaster Name: _____   Wait Time: _____

Park Area: _____   Ticket Price: _____

Weather: _____   Express Pass: Yes   No

Crowd: _____

Coaster Manufacturer: _____

Coaster Type: Wood   Steel   Hyper   Hybrid   Converted

Coaster Design: (circle all applicable options)

4th Dimension	Accelerator	Bobsled	Dive	Flying	Floorless
Inverted	Mine Train	Motorbike	Pipeline		Side Friction
Single Rail	Sit Down	Spinning	Stand Up	Suspended	Wing

Restraint Type:

Lap Bar   Lap Bar w/seatbelt   Shoulder Harness   Motorbike

Shoulder Harness w/seatbelt   Vest Harness

Other:

Coaster Stats

Height:	Number of Inversions:
Length:	Duration:
Speed:	Cars Per Train:
Drop:	Height Restrictions: min: max:

Other Restrictions: (i.e. lockers required, metal detector, etc.)

My Rating: ☆ ☆ ☆ ☆ ☆   Seat Location: Front   Middle   Back

My Review:

Theme Park: _____ Date: _____

Location: _____ First Ride: Yes   No

Coaster Name: _____ Wait Time: _____

Park Area: _____ Ticket Price: _____

Weather: _____ Express Pass: Yes   No

Crowd: _____

Coaster Manufacturer: _____

Coaster Type: Wood   Steel   Hyper   Hybrid   Converted

Coaster Design: (circle all applicable options)

4th Dimension	Accelerator	Bobsled	Dive	Flying	Floorless
Inverted	Mine Train	Motorbike		Pipeline	Side Friction
Single Rail	Sit Down	Spinning	Stand Up	Suspended	Wing

Restraint Type:

Lap Bar   Lap Bar w/seatbelt   Shoulder Harness   Motorbike

Shoulder Harness w/seatbelt   Vest Harness

Other: _____

Coaster Stats

Height:	Number of Inversions:
Length:	Duration:
Speed:	Cars Per Train:
Drop:	Height Restrictions: min: max:

Other Restrictions: (i.e. lockers required, metal detector, etc.)

My Rating: ☆ ☆ ☆ ☆ ☆   Seat Location: Front   Middle   Back

My Review:

Theme Park: _____ Date: _____

Location: _____ First Ride: Yes No

Coaster Name: _____ Wait Time: _____

Park Area: _____ Ticket Price: _____

Weather: _____ Express Pass: Yes No

Crowd: _____

Coaster Manufacturer: _____

Coaster Type: Wood   Steel   Hyper   Hybrid   Converted

Coaster Design: (circle all applicable options)

4th Dimension	Accelerator	Bobsled	Dive	Flying	Floorless
Inverted	Mine Train	Motorbike		Pipeline	Side Friction
Single Rail	Sit Down	Spinning	Stand Up	Suspended	Wing

Restraint Type:

Lap Bar	Lap Bar w/seatbelt	Shoulder Harness	Motorbike
Shoulder Harness w/seatbelt	Vest Harness	
Other:		

Coaster Stats

Height:	Number of Inversions:
Length:	Duration:
Speed:	Cars Per Train:
Drop:	Height Restrictions: min: max:

Other Restrictions: (i.e. lockers required, metal detector, etc.)

_____

My Rating: ☆ ☆ ☆ ☆ ☆   Seat Location: Front Middle Back

My Review:

Theme Park: _____ Date: _____

Location: _____ First Ride: Yes   No

Coaster Name: _____ Wait Time: _____

Park Area: _____ Ticket Price: _____

Weather: _____ Express Pass: Yes   No

Crowd: _____

Coaster Manufacturer: _____

Coaster Type: Wood   Steel   Hyper   Hybrid   Converted

Coaster Design: (circle all applicable options)

4th Dimension	Accelerator	Bobsled	Dive	Flying	Floorless
Inverted	Mine Train	Motorbike	Pipeline		Side Friction
Single Rail	Sit Down	Spinning	Stand Up	Suspended	Wing

Restraint Type:

Lap Bar   Lap Bar w/seatbelt   Shoulder Harness   Motorbike

Shoulder Harness w/seatbelt   Vest Harness

Other: _____

Coaster Stats

Height:	Number of Inversions:
Length:	Duration:
Speed:	Cars Per Train:
Drop:	Height Restrictions: min: max:

Other Restrictions: (i.e. lockers required, metal detector, etc.)

My Rating: ☆ ☆ ☆ ☆ ☆   Seat Location: Front   Middle   Back

My Review:

Theme Park: _____ Date: _____

Location: _____ First Ride: Yes   No

Coaster Name: _____ Wait Time: _____

Park Area: _____ Ticket Price: _____

Weather: _____ Express Pass: Yes   No

Crowd: _____

Coaster Manufacturer: _____

Coaster Type: Wood   Steel   Hyper   Hybrid   Converted

Coaster Design: (circle all applicable options)

4th Dimension	Accelerator	Bobsled	Dive	Flying	Floorless
Inverted	Mine Train	Motorbike	Pipeline		Side Friction
Single Rail	Sit Down	Spinning	Stand Up	Suspended	Wing

Restraint Type:

Lap Bar   Lap Bar w/seatbelt   Shoulder Harness   Motorbike

Shoulder Harness w/seatbelt   Vest Harness

Other: _____

Coaster Stats

Height:	Number of Inversions:
Length:	Duration:
Speed:	Cars Per Train:
Drop:	Height Restrictions: min: max:

Other Restrictions: (i.e. lockers required, metal detector, etc.)

My Rating: ☆ ☆ ☆ ☆ ☆   Seat Location: Front   Middle   Back

My Review:

Theme Park: _____   Date: _____

Location: _____   First Ride: Yes   No

Coaster Name: _____   Wait Time: _____

Park Area: _____   Ticket Price: _____

Weather: _____   Express Pass: Yes   No

Crowd: _____

Coaster Manufacturer: _____

Coaster Type: Wood   Steel   Hyper   Hybrid   Converted

Coaster Design: (circle all applicable options)

4th Dimension	Accelerator	Bobsled	Dive	Flying	Floorless
Inverted	Mine Train	Motorbike		Pipeline	Side Friction
Single Rail	Sit Down	Spinning	Stand Up	Suspended	Wing

Restraint Type:

Lap Bar   Lap Bar w/seatbelt   Shoulder Harness   Motorbike

Shoulder Harness w/seatbelt   Vest Harness

Other: _____

Coaster Stats

Height:	Number of Inversions:
Length:	Duration:
Speed:	Cars Per Train:
Drop:	Height Restrictions: min: max:

Other Restrictions: (i.e. lockers required, metal detector, etc.)

My Rating: ☆ ☆ ☆ ☆ ☆   Seat Location: Front   Middle   Back

My Review:

Theme Park: _____   Date: _____

Location: _____   First Ride: Yes   No

Coaster Name: _____   Wait Time: _____

Park Area: _____   Ticket Price: _____

Weather: _____   Express Pass: Yes No

Crowd: _____

Coaster Manufacturer: _____

Coaster Type: Wood   Steel   Hyper   Hybrid   Converted

Coaster Design: (circle all applicable options)

4th Dimension	Accelerator	Bobsled	Dive	Flying	Floorless
Inverted	Mine Train	Motorbike	Pipeline		Side Friction
Single Rail	Sit Down	Spinning	Stand Up	Suspended	Wing

Restraint Type:

Lap Bar	Lap Bar w/seatbelt	Shoulder Harness	Motorbike
Shoulder Harness w/seatbelt		Vest Harness	
Other:			

Coaster Stats

Height:	Number of Inversions:
Length:	Duration:
Speed:	Cars Per Train:
Drop:	Height Restrictions: min: max:

Other Restrictions: (i.e. lockers required, metal detector, etc.)

My Rating: ☆☆☆☆☆   Seat Location: Front   Middle   Back

My Review:

Theme Park: _____   Date: _____

Location: _____   First Ride: Yes   No

Coaster Name: _____   Wait Time: _____

Park Area: _____   Ticket Price: _____

Weather: _____   Express Pass: Yes   No

Crowd: _____

Coaster Manufacturer: _____

Coaster Type: Wood   Steel   Hyper   Hybrid   Converted

Coaster Design: (circle all applicable options)

4th Dimension	Accelerator	Bobsled	Dive	Flying	Floorless
Inverted	Mine Train	Motorbike	Pipeline		Side Friction
Single Rail	Sit Down	Spinning	Stand Up	Suspended	Wing

Restraint Type:

Lap Bar	Lap Bar w/seatbelt	Shoulder Harness	Motorbike
Shoulder Harness w/seatbelt		Vest Harness	
Other:			

Coaster Stats

Height:	Number of Inversions:
Length:	Duration:
Speed:	Cars Per Train:
Drop:	Height Restrictions: min: max:

Other Restrictions: (i.e. lockers required, metal detector, etc.)

My Rating: ☆ ☆ ☆ ☆ ☆   Seat Location: Front   Middle   Back

My Review:

Theme Park: _____ Date: _____

Location: _____ First Ride: Yes   No

Coaster Name: _____ Wait Time: _____

Park Area: _____ Ticket Price: _____

Weather: _____ Express Pass: Yes No

Crowd: _____

Coaster Manufacturer: _____

Coaster Type: Wood   Steel   Hyper   Hybrid   Converted

Coaster Design: (circle all applicable options)

4th Dimension	Accelerator	Bobsled	Dive	Flying	Floorless
Inverted	Mine Train	Motorbike	Pipeline		Side Friction
Single Rail	Sit Down	Spinning	Stand Up	Suspended	Wing

Restraint Type:

Lap Bar   Lap Bar w/seatbelt   Shoulder Harness   Motorbike

Shoulder Harness w/seatbelt   Vest Harness

Other:

Coaster Stats

Height:	Number of Inversions:
Length:	Duration:
Speed:	Cars Per Train:
Drop:	Height Restrictions: min: max:

Other Restrictions: (i.e. lockers required, metal detector, etc.)

My Rating: ☆ ☆ ☆ ☆ ☆   Seat Location: Front   Middle   Back

My Review:

Theme Park: _____   Date: _____

Location: _____   First Ride: Yes   No

Coaster Name: _____   Wait Time: _____

Park Area: _____   Ticket Price: _____

Weather: _____   Express Pass: Yes   No

Crowd: _____

Coaster Manufacturer: _____

Coaster Type: Wood   Steel   Hyper   Hybrid   Converted

Coaster Design: (circle all applicable options)

4th Dimension	Accelerator	Bobsled	Dive	Flying	Floorless
Inverted	Mine Train	Motorbike	Pipeline		Side Friction
Single Rail	Sit Down	Spinning	Stand Up	Suspended	Wing

Restraint Type:

Lap Bar   Lap Bar w/seatbelt   Shoulder Harness   Motorbike

Shoulder Harness w/seatbelt   Vest Harness

Other:

Coaster Stats

Height:	Number of Inversions:
Length:	Duration:
Speed:	Cars Per Train:
Drop:	Height Restrictions: min: max:

Other Restrictions: (i.e. lockers required, metal detector, etc.)

My Rating: ☆ ☆ ☆ ☆ ☆   Seat Location: Front   Middle   Back

My Review:

Theme Park: _____   Date: _____

Location: _____   First Ride: Yes   No

Coaster Name: _____   Wait Time: _____

Park Area: _____   Ticket Price: _____

Weather: _____   Express Pass: Yes   No

Crowd: _____

Coaster Manufacturer: _____

Coaster Type: Wood   Steel   Hyper   Hybrid   Converted

Coaster Design: (circle all applicable options)

4th Dimension	Accelerator	Bobsled	Dive	Flying	Floorless
Inverted	Mine Train	Motorbike	Pipeline		Side Friction
Single Rail	Sit Down	Spinning	Stand Up	Suspended	Wing

Restraint Type:

Lap Bar   Lap Bar w/seatbelt   Shoulder Harness   Motorbike

Shoulder Harness w/seatbelt   Vest Harness

Other:

Coaster Stats

Height:	Number of Inversions:
Length:	Duration:
Speed:	Cars Per Train:
Drop:	Height Restrictions: min: max:

Other Restrictions: (i.e. lockers required, metal detector, etc.)

My Rating: ☆ ☆ ☆ ☆ ☆   Seat Location: Front   Middle   Back

My Review:

Theme Park: _____ Date: _____

Location: _____ First Ride: Yes   No

Coaster Name: _____ Wait Time: _____

Park Area: _____ Ticket Price: _____

Weather: _____ Express Pass: Yes   No

Crowd: _____

Coaster Manufacturer: _____

Coaster Type: Wood   Steel   Hyper   Hybrid   Converted

Coaster Design: (circle all applicable options)

4th Dimension	Accelerator	Bobsled	Dive	Flying	Floorless
Inverted	Mine Train	Motorbike	Pipeline		Side Friction
Single Rail	Sit Down	Spinning	Stand Up	Suspended	Wing

Restraint Type:

Lap Bar	Lap Bar w/seatbelt	Shoulder Harness	Motorbike
Shoulder Harness w/seatbelt		Vest Harness	
Other:			

Coaster Stats

Height:	Number of Inversions:
Length:	Duration:
Speed:	Cars Per Train:
Drop:	Height Restrictions: min: max:

Other Restrictions: (i.e. lockers required, metal detector, etc.)

My Rating: ☆ ☆ ☆ ☆ ☆   Seat Location: Front   Middle   Back

My Review:

Theme Park: _____ Date: _____

Location: _____ First Ride: Yes   No

Coaster Name: _____ Wait Time: _____

Park Area: _____ Ticket Price: _____

Weather: _____ Express Pass: Yes   No

Crowd: _____

Coaster Manufacturer: _____

Coaster Type: Wood   Steel   Hyper   Hybrid   Converted

Coaster Design: (circle all applicable options)

4th Dimension	Accelerator	Bobsled	Dive	Flying	Floorless
Inverted	Mine Train	Motorbike	Pipeline		Side Friction
Single Rail	Sit Down	Spinning	Stand Up	Suspended	Wing

Restraint Type:

Lap Bar   Lap Bar w/seatbelt   Shoulder Harness   Motorbike

Shoulder Harness w/seatbelt   Vest Harness

Other:

Coaster Stats

Height:	Number of Inversions:
Length:	Duration:
Speed:	Cars Per Train:
Drop:	Height Restrictions: min: max:

Other Restrictions: (i.e. lockers required, metal detector, etc.)

My Rating: ☆ ☆ ☆ ☆ ☆   Seat Location: Front   Middle   Back

My Review:

Theme Park: _____   Date: _____

Location: _____   First Ride: Yes   No

Coaster Name: _____   Wait Time: _____

Park Area: _____   Ticket Price: _____

Weather: _____   Express Pass: Yes   No

Crowd: _____

Coaster Manufacturer: _____

Coaster Type: Wood   Steel   Hyper   Hybrid   Converted

Coaster Design: (circle all applicable options)

4th Dimension	Accelerator	Bobsled	Dive	Flying	Floorless
Inverted	Mine Train	Motorbike		Pipeline	Side Friction
Single Rail	Sit Down	Spinning	Stand Up	Suspended	Wing

Restraint Type:

Lap Bar	Lap Bar w/seatbelt	Shoulder Harness	Motorbike
Shoulder Harness w/seatbelt		Vest Harness	
Other:			

Coaster Stats

Height:	Number of Inversions:
Length:	Duration:
Speed:	Cars Per Train:
Drop:	Height Restrictions: min: max:

Other Restrictions: (i.e. lockers required, metal detector, etc.)

_____

My Rating: ☆ ☆ ☆ ☆ ☆   Seat Location: Front   Middle   Back

My Review:

_____

88

Theme Park:	Date:
Location:	First Ride: Yes No
Coaster Name:	Wait Time:
Park Area:	Ticket Price:
Weather:	Express Pass: Yes No
Crowd:	

Coaster Manufacturer:

Coaster Type: Wood   Steel   Hyper   Hybrid   Converted

Coaster Design: (circle all applicable options)

4th Dimension	Accelerator	Bobsled	Dive	Flying	Floorless
Inverted	Mine Train	Motorbike	Pipeline		Side Friction
Single Rail	Sit Down	Spinning	Stand Up	Suspended	Wing

Restraint Type:

Lap Bar   Lap Bar w/seatbelt   Shoulder Harness   Motorbike

Shoulder Harness w/seatbelt   Vest Harness

Other:

Coaster Stats

Height:	Number of Inversions:
Length:	Duration:
Speed:	Cars Per Train:
Drop:	Height Restrictions: min: max:

Other Restrictions: (i.e. lockers required, metal detector, etc.)

My Rating: ☆ ☆ ☆ ☆ ☆   Seat Location: Front   Middle   Back

My Review:

Theme Park: _____   Date: _____

Location: _____   First Ride: Yes   No

Coaster Name: _____   Wait Time: _____

Park Area: _____   Ticket Price: _____

Weather: _____   Express Pass: Yes   No

Crowd: _____

Coaster Manufacturer: _____

Coaster Type: Wood   Steel   Hyper   Hybrid   Converted

Coaster Design: (circle all applicable options)

4th Dimension	Accelerator	Bobsled	Dive	Flying	Floorless
Inverted	Mine Train	Motorbike	Pipeline		Side Friction
Single Rail	Sit Down	Spinning	Stand Up	Suspended	Wing

Restraint Type:

Lap Bar   Lap Bar w/seatbelt   Shoulder Harness   Motorbike

Shoulder Harness w/seatbelt   Vest Harness

Other: _____

Coaster Stats

Height:	Number of Inversions:
Length:	Duration:
Speed:	Cars Per Train:
Drop:	Height Restrictions: min: max:

Other Restrictions: (i.e. lockers required, metal detector, etc.)

My Rating: ☆ ☆ ☆ ☆ ☆   Seat Location: Front   Middle   Back

My Review:

Theme Park: _____   Date: _____

Location: _____   First Ride: Yes   No

Coaster Name: _____   Wait Time: _____

Park Area: _____   Ticket Price: _____

Weather: _____   Express Pass: Yes No

Crowd: _____

Coaster Manufacturer: _____

Coaster Type: Wood   Steel   Hyper   Hybrid   Converted

Coaster Design: (circle all applicable options)

4th Dimension	Accelerator	Bobsled	Dive	Flying	Floorless
Inverted	Mine Train	Motorbike	Pipeline		Side Friction
Single Rail	Sit Down	Spinning	Stand Up	Suspended	Wing

Restraint Type:

Lap Bar	Lap Bar w/seatbelt	Shoulder Harness	Motorbike
Shoulder Harness w/seatbelt		Vest Harness	
Other:			

Coaster Stats

Height:	Number of Inversions:
Length:	Duration:
Speed:	Cars Per Train:
Drop:	Height Restrictions: min: max:

Other Restrictions: (i.e. lockers required, metal detector, etc.)

My Rating: ☆ ☆ ☆ ☆ ☆   Seat Location: Front   Middle   Back

My Review:

Theme Park: _____ Date: _____

Location: _____ First Ride: Yes   No

Coaster Name: _____ Wait Time: _____

Park Area: _____ Ticket Price: _____

Weather: _____ Express Pass: Yes   No

Crowd: _____

Coaster Manufacturer: _____

Coaster Type: Wood   Steel   Hyper   Hybrid   Converted

Coaster Design: (circle all applicable options)

4th Dimension	Accelerator	Bobsled	Dive	Flying	Floorless
Inverted	Mine Train	Motorbike	Pipeline		Side Friction
Single Rail	Sit Down	Spinning	Stand Up	Suspended	Wing

Restraint Type:

Lap Bar   Lap Bar w/seatbelt   Shoulder Harness   Motorbike

Shoulder Harness w/seatbelt   Vest Harness

Other:

Coaster Stats

Height:	Number of Inversions:
Length:	Duration:
Speed:	Cars Per Train:
Drop:	Height Restrictions: min: max:

Other Restrictions: (i.e. lockers required, metal detector, etc.)

My Rating: ☆☆☆☆☆   Seat Location: Front   Middle   Back

My Review:

Theme Park: _____ Date: _____

Location: _____ First Ride: Yes   No

Coaster Name: _____ Wait Time: _____

Park Area: _____ Ticket Price: _____

Weather: _____ Express Pass: Yes No

Crowd: _____

Coaster Manufacturer: _____

Coaster Type: Wood   Steel   Hyper   Hybrid   Converted

Coaster Design: (circle all applicable options)

4th Dimension	Accelerator	Bobsled	Dive	Flying	Floorless
Inverted	Mine Train	Motorbike	Pipeline		Side Friction
Single Rail	Sit Down	Spinning	Stand Up	Suspended	Wing

Restraint Type:

Lap Bar   Lap Bar w/seatbelt   Shoulder Harness   Motorbike

Shoulder Harness w/seatbelt   Vest Harness

Other: _____

Coaster Stats

Height:	Number of Inversions:
Length:	Duration:
Speed:	Cars Per Train:
Drop:	Height Restrictions: min: max:

Other Restrictions: (i.e. lockers required, metal detector, etc.)

My Rating: ☆ ☆ ☆ ☆ ☆   Seat Location: Front   Middle   Back

My Review:

Theme Park: _____   Date: _____

Location: _____   First Ride: Yes   No

Coaster Name: _____   Wait Time: _____

Park Area: _____   Ticket Price: _____

Weather: _____   Express Pass: Yes   No

Crowd: _____

Coaster Manufacturer: _____

Coaster Type: Wood   Steel   Hyper   Hybrid   Converted

Coaster Design: (circle all applicable options)

4th Dimension	Accelerator	Bobsled	Dive	Flying	Floorless
Inverted	Mine Train	Motorbike	Pipeline		Side Friction
Single Rail	Sit Down	Spinning	Stand Up	Suspended	Wing

Restraint Type:

Lap Bar	Lap Bar w/seatbelt	Shoulder Harness	Motorbike
Shoulder Harness w/seatbelt		Vest Harness	
Other:			

Coaster Stats

Height:	Number of Inversions:
Length:	Duration:
Speed:	Cars Per Train:
Drop:	Height Restrictions: min: max:

Other Restrictions: (i.e. lockers required, metal detector, etc.)

My Rating: ☆ ☆ ☆ ☆ ☆   Seat Location: Front   Middle   Back

My Review:

94

Theme Park: _____ Date: _____

Location: _____ First Ride: Yes   No

Coaster Name: _____ Wait Time: _____

Park Area: _____ Ticket Price: _____

Weather: _____ Express Pass: Yes No

Crowd: _____

Coaster Manufacturer: _____

Coaster Type: Wood   Steel   Hyper   Hybrid   Converted

Coaster Design: (circle all applicable options)

4th Dimension	Accelerator	Bobsled	Dive	Flying	Floorless
Inverted	Mine Train	Motorbike	Pipeline		Side Friction
Single Rail	Sit Down	Spinning	Stand Up	Suspended	Wing

Restraint Type: _____

Lap Bar   Lap Bar w/seatbelt   Shoulder Harness   Motorbike

Shoulder Harness w/seatbelt   Vest Harness

Other: _____

Coaster Stats

Height:	Number of Inversions:
Length:	Duration:
Speed:	Cars Per Train:
Drop:	Height Restrictions: min: max:

Other Restrictions: (i.e. lockers required, metal detector, etc.)

_____

My Rating: ☆ ☆ ☆ ☆ ☆   Seat Location: Front   Middle   Back

My Review:

_____

Theme Park: _____ Date: _____

Location: _____ First Ride: Yes No

Coaster Name: _____ Wait Time: _____

Park Area: _____ Ticket Price: _____

Weather: _____ Express Pass: Yes No

Crowd: _____

Coaster Manufacturer: _____

Coaster Type: Wood   Steel   Hyper   Hybrid   Converted

Coaster Design: (circle all applicable options)

4th Dimension	Accelerator	Bobsled	Dive	Flying	Floorless
Inverted	Mine Train	Motorbike	Pipeline		Side Friction
Single Rail	Sit Down	Spinning	Stand Up	Suspended	Wing

Restraint Type:

Lap Bar   Lap Bar w/seatbelt   Shoulder Harness   Motorbike

Shoulder Harness w/seatbelt   Vest Harness

Other:

Coaster Stats

Height:	Number of Inversions:
Length:	Duration:
Speed:	Cars Per Train:
Drop:	Height Restrictions: min: max:

Other Restrictions: (i.e. lockers required, metal detector, etc.)

My Rating: ☆ ☆ ☆ ☆ ☆   Seat Location: Front Middle Back

My Review:

Theme Park: _____   Date: _____

Location: _____   First Ride: Yes   No

Coaster Name: _____   Wait Time: _____

Park Area: _____   Ticket Price: _____

Weather: _____   Express Pass: Yes   No

Crowd: _____

Coaster Manufacturer: _____

Coaster Type: Wood   Steel   Hyper   Hybrid   Converted

Coaster Design: (circle all applicable options)

4th Dimension	Accelerator	Bobsled	Dive	Flying	Floorless
Inverted	Mine Train	Motorbike	Pipeline		Side Friction
Single Rail	Sit Down	Spinning	Stand Up	Suspended	Wing

Restraint Type:

Lap Bar	Lap Bar w/seatbelt	Shoulder Harness	Motorbike
Shoulder Harness w/seatbelt		Vest Harness	
Other:			

Coaster Stats

Height:	Number of Inversions:
Length:	Duration:
Speed:	Cars Per Train:
Drop:	Height Restrictions: min: max:

Other Restrictions: (i.e. lockers required, metal detector, etc.)

My Rating: ☆ ☆ ☆ ☆ ☆   Seat Location: Front   Middle   Back

My Review:

Theme Park: _____ Date: _____

Location: _____ First Ride: Yes   No

Coaster Name: _____ Wait Time: _____

Park Area: _____ Ticket Price: _____

Weather: _____ Express Pass: Yes   No

Crowd: _____

Coaster Manufacturer: _____

Coaster Type: Wood   Steel   Hyper   Hybrid   Converted

Coaster Design: (circle all applicable options)

4th Dimension	Accelerator	Bobsled	Dive	Flying	Floorless
Inverted	Mine Train	Motorbike	Pipeline		Side Friction
Single Rail	Sit Down	Spinning	Stand Up	Suspended	Wing

Restraint Type:

Lap Bar   Lap Bar w/seatbelt   Shoulder Harness   Motorbike

Shoulder Harness w/seatbelt   Vest Harness

Other:

Coaster Stats

Height:	Number of Inversions:
Length:	Duration:
Speed:	Cars Per Train:
Drop:	Height Restrictions: min: max:

Other Restrictions: (i.e. lockers required, metal detector, etc.)

My Rating: ☆ ☆ ☆ ☆ ☆   Seat Location: Front   Middle   Back

My Review:

Theme Park: _____   Date: _____

Location: _____   First Ride: Yes   No

Coaster Name: _____   Wait Time: _____

Park Area: _____   Ticket Price: _____

Weather: _____   Express Pass: Yes   No

Crowd: _____

Coaster Manufacturer: _____

Coaster Type: Wood   Steel   Hyper   Hybrid   Converted

Coaster Design: (circle all applicable options)

4th Dimension	Accelerator	Bobsled	Dive	Flying	Floorless
Inverted	Mine Train	Motorbike	Pipeline		Side Friction
Single Rail	Sit Down	Spinning	Stand Up	Suspended	Wing

Restraint Type:

Lap Bar   Lap Bar w/seatbelt   Shoulder Harness   Motorbike
Shoulder Harness w/seatbelt   Vest Harness
Other:

Coaster Stats

Height:	Number of Inversions:
Length:	Duration:
Speed:	Cars Per Train:
Drop:	Height Restrictions: min: max:

Other Restrictions: (i.e. lockers required, metal detector, etc.)

My Rating: ☆☆☆☆☆   Seat Location: Front   Middle   Back

My Review:

Theme Park: _____ Date: _____

Location: _____ First Ride: Yes   No

Coaster Name: _____ Wait Time: _____

Park Area: _____ Ticket Price: _____

Weather: _____ Express Pass: Yes   No

Crowd: _____

Coaster Manufacturer: _____

Coaster Type: Wood   Steel   Hyper   Hybrid   Converted

Coaster Design: (circle all applicable options)

4th Dimension	Accelerator	Bobsled	Dive	Flying	Floorless
Inverted	Mine Train	Motorbike		Pipeline	Side Friction
Single Rail	Sit Down	Spinning	Stand Up	Suspended	Wing

Restraint Type:

Lap Bar	Lap Bar w/seatbelt	Shoulder Harness	Motorbike
Shoulder Harness w/seatbelt		Vest Harness	
Other:			

Coaster Stats

Height:	Number of Inversions:
Length:	Duration:
Speed:	Cars Per Train:
Drop:	Height Restrictions: min: max:

Other Restrictions: (i.e. lockers required, metal detector, etc.)

My Rating: ☆ ☆ ☆ ☆ ☆   Seat Location: Front   Middle   Back

My Review:

100

Theme Park: _____ Date: _____

Location: _____ First Ride: Yes No

Coaster Name: _____ Wait Time: _____

Park Area: _____ Ticket Price: _____

Weather: _____ Express Pass: Yes No

Crowd: _____

Coaster Manufacturer: _____

Coaster Type: Wood   Steel   Hyper   Hybrid   Converted

Coaster Design: (circle all applicable options)

4th Dimension	Accelerator	Bobsled	Dive	Flying	Floorless
Inverted	Mine Train	Motorbike	Pipeline		Side Friction
Single Rail	Sit Down	Spinning	Stand Up	Suspended	Wing

Restraint Type:

Lap Bar   Lap Bar w/seatbelt   Shoulder Harness   Motorbike

Shoulder Harness w/seatbelt   Vest Harness

Other: _____

Coaster Stats

Height:	Number of Inversions:
Length:	Duration:
Speed:	Cars Per Train:
Drop:	Height Restrictions: min: max:

Other Restrictions: (i.e. lockers required, metal detector, etc.)

_____

My Rating: ☆ ☆ ☆ ☆ ☆   Seat Location: Front   Middle   Back

My Review:

_____

Theme Park: _____ Date: _____

Location: _____ First Ride: Yes   No

Coaster Name: _____ Wait Time: _____

Park Area: _____ Ticket Price: _____

Weather: _____ Express Pass: Yes   No

Crowd: _____

Coaster Manufacturer: _____

Coaster Type: Wood   Steel   Hyper   Hybrid   Converted

Coaster Design: (circle all applicable options)

4th Dimension	Accelerator	Bobsled	Dive	Flying	Floorless
Inverted	Mine Train	Motorbike	Pipeline		Side Friction
Single Rail	Sit Down	Spinning	Stand Up	Suspended	Wing

Restraint Type:

Lap Bar   Lap Bar w/seatbelt   Shoulder Harness   Motorbike

Shoulder Harness w/seatbelt   Vest Harness

Other: _____

Coaster Stats

Height:	Number of Inversions:
Length:	Duration:
Speed:	Cars Per Train:
Drop:	Height Restrictions: min: max:

Other Restrictions: (i.e. lockers required, metal detector, etc.)

My Rating: ☆ ☆ ☆ ☆ ☆   Seat Location: Front   Middle   Back

My Review:

Theme Park: _____   Date: _____

Location: _____   First Ride: Yes   No

Coaster Name: _____   Wait Time: _____

Park Area: _____   Ticket Price: _____

Weather: _____   Express Pass: Yes   No

Crowd: _____

Coaster Manufacturer: _____

Coaster Type: Wood   Steel   Hyper   Hybrid   Converted

Coaster Design: (circle all applicable options)

4th Dimension	Accelerator	Bobsled	Dive	Flying	Floorless
Inverted	Mine Train	Motorbike	Pipeline		Side Friction
Single Rail	Sit Down	Spinning	Stand Up	Suspended	Wing

Restraint Type:

Lap Bar	Lap Bar w/seatbelt	Shoulder Harness	Motorbike
Shoulder Harness w/seatbelt		Vest Harness	
Other:			

Coaster Stats

Height:	Number of Inversions:
Length:	Duration:
Speed:	Cars Per Train:
Drop:	Height Restrictions: min: max:

Other Restrictions: (i.e. lockers required, metal detector, etc.)

My Rating: ☆ ☆ ☆ ☆ ☆   Seat Location: Front   Middle   Back

My Review:

Theme Park: _____ Date: _____

Location: _____ First Ride: Yes   No

Coaster Name: _____ Wait Time: _____

Park Area: _____ Ticket Price: _____

Weather: _____ Express Pass: Yes   No

Crowd: _____

Coaster Manufacturer: _____

Coaster Type: Wood   Steel   Hyper   Hybrid   Converted

Coaster Design: (circle all applicable options)

4th Dimension	Accelerator	Bobsled	Dive	Flying	Floorless
Inverted	Mine Train	Motorbike	Pipeline		Side Friction
Single Rail	Sit Down	Spinning	Stand Up	Suspended	Wing

Restraint Type:

Lap Bar   Lap Bar w/seatbelt   Shoulder Harness   Motorbike

Shoulder Harness w/seatbelt   Vest Harness

Other:

Coaster Stats

Height:	Number of Inversions:
Length:	Duration:
Speed:	Cars Per Train:
Drop:	Height Restrictions: min: max:

Other Restrictions: (i.e. lockers required, metal detector, etc.)

My Rating: ☆ ☆ ☆ ☆ ☆   Seat Location: Front   Middle   Back

My Review:

104

Theme Park: _____   Date: _____

Location: _____   First Ride: Yes   No

Coaster Name: _____   Wait Time: _____

Park Area: _____   Ticket Price: _____

Weather: _____   Express Pass: Yes   No

Crowd: _____

Coaster Manufacturer: _____

Coaster Type: Wood   Steel   Hyper   Hybrid   Converted

Coaster Design: (circle all applicable options)

4th Dimension	Accelerator	Bobsled	Dive	Flying	Floorless
Inverted	Mine Train	Motorbike	Pipeline		Side Friction
Single Rail	Sit Down	Spinning	Stand Up	Suspended	Wing

Restraint Type:

Lap Bar	Lap Bar w/seatbelt	Shoulder Harness Motorbike
Shoulder Harness w/seatbelt	Vest Harness	
Other:		

Coaster Stats

Height:	Number of Inversions:
Length:	Duration:
Speed:	Cars Per Train:
Drop:	Height Restrictions: min: max:

Other Restrictions: (i.e. lockers required, metal detector, etc.)

My Rating: ☆☆☆☆☆   Seat Location: Front   Middle   Back

My Review:

Theme Park: _____   Date: _____

Location: _____   First Ride: Yes   No

Coaster Name: _____   Wait Time: _____

Park Area: _____   Ticket Price: _____

Weather: _____   Express Pass: Yes   No

Crowd: _____

Coaster Manufacturer: _____

Coaster Type: Wood   Steel   Hyper   Hybrid   Converted

Coaster Design: (circle all applicable options)

4th Dimension	Accelerator	Bobsled	Dive	Flying	Floorless
Inverted	Mine Train	Motorbike		Pipeline	Side Friction
Single Rail	Sit Down	Spinning	Stand Up	Suspended	Wing

Restraint Type:

Lap Bar   Lap Bar w/seatbelt   Shoulder Harness   Motorbike

Shoulder Harness w/seatbelt   Vest Harness

Other: _____

Coaster Stats

Height:	Number of Inversions:
Length:	Duration:
Speed:	Cars Per Train:
Drop:	Height Restrictions: min: max:

Other Restrictions: (i.e. lockers required, metal detector, etc.)

_____

My Rating: ☆ ☆ ☆ ☆ ☆   Seat Location: Front   Middle   Back

My Review:

_____

Theme Park: _____ Date: _____

Location: _____ First Ride: Yes   No

Coaster Name: _____ Wait Time: _____

Park Area: _____ Ticket Price: _____

Weather: _____ Express Pass: Yes   No

Crowd: _____

Coaster Manufacturer: _____

Coaster Type: Wood   Steel   Hyper   Hybrid   Converted

Coaster Design: (circle all applicable options)

4th Dimension	Accelerator	Bobsled	Dive	Flying	Floorless
Inverted	Mine Train	Motorbike	Pipeline		Side Friction
Single Rail	Sit Down	Spinning	Stand Up	Suspended	Wing

Restraint Type:

Lap Bar   Lap Bar w/seatbelt   Shoulder Harness   Motorbike

Shoulder Harness w/seatbelt   Vest Harness

Other: _____

Coaster Stats

Height:	Number of Inversions:
Length:	Duration:
Speed:	Cars Per Train:
Drop:	Height Restrictions: min: max:

Other Restrictions: (i.e. lockers required, metal detector, etc.)

My Rating: ☆☆☆☆☆   Seat Location: Front   Middle   Back

My Review:

Theme Park: | Date:

Location: | First Ride: Yes   No

Coaster Name: | Wait Time:

Park Area: | Ticket Price:

Weather: | Express Pass: Yes   No

Crowd:

Coaster Manufacturer:

Coaster Type: Wood   Steel   Hyper   Hybrid   Converted

Coaster Design: (circle all applicable options)

| 4th Dimension   Accelerator   Bobsled   Dive   Flying   Floorless |
| Inverted   Mine Train   Motorbike   Pipeline   Side Friction |
| Single Rail   Sit Down   Spinning   Stand Up   Suspended   Wing |

Restraint Type:

| Lap Bar   Lap Bar w/seatbelt   Shoulder Harness   Motorbike |
| Shoulder Harness w/seatbelt   Vest Harness |
| Other: |

Coaster Stats

Height:	Number of Inversions:
Length:	Duration:
Speed:	Cars Per Train:
Drop:	Height Restrictions: min: max:

Other Restrictions: (i.e. lockers required, metal detector, etc.)

My Rating: ☆☆☆☆☆   Seat Location: Front   Middle   Back

My Review:

Theme Park: _____ Date: _____

Location: _____ First Ride: Yes   No

Coaster Name: _____ Wait Time: _____

Park Area: _____ Ticket Price: _____

Weather: _____ Express Pass: Yes   No

Crowd: _____

Coaster Manufacturer: _____

Coaster Type: Wood   Steel   Hyper   Hybrid   Converted

Coaster Design: (circle all applicable options)

4th Dimension	Accelerator	Bobsled	Dive	Flying	Floorless
Inverted	Mine Train	Motorbike	Pipeline		Side Friction
Single Rail	Sit Down	Spinning	Stand Up	Suspended	Wing

Restraint Type:

Lap Bar Lap Bar w/seatbelt Shoulder Harness Motorbike	
Shoulder Harness w/seatbelt Vest Harness	
Other:	

Coaster Stats

Height:	Number of Inversions:
Length:	Duration:
Speed:	Cars Per Train:
Drop:	Height Restrictions: min: max:

Other Restrictions: (i.e. lockers required, metal detector, etc.)

My Rating: ☆☆☆☆☆   Seat Location: Front   Middle   Back

My Review:

Theme Park: _____ Date: _____

Location: _____ First Ride: Yes   No

Coaster Name: _____ Wait Time: _____

Park Area: _____ Ticket Price: _____

Weather: _____ Express Pass: Yes   No

Crowd: _____

Coaster Manufacturer: _____

Coaster Type: Wood   Steel   Hyper   Hybrid   Converted

Coaster Design: (circle all applicable options)

4th Dimension	Accelerator	Bobsled	Dive	Flying	Floorless
Inverted	Mine Train	Motorbike	Pipeline		Side Friction
Single Rail	Sit Down	Spinning	Stand Up	Suspended	Wing

Restraint Type:

Lap Bar   Lap Bar w/seatbelt   Shoulder Harness   Motorbike

Shoulder Harness w/seatbelt   Vest Harness

Other:

Coaster Stats

Height:	Number of Inversions:
Length:	Duration:
Speed:	Cars Per Train:
Drop:	Height Restrictions: min: max:

Other Restrictions: (i.e. lockers required, metal detector, etc.)

My Rating: ☆ ☆ ☆ ☆ ☆   Seat Location: Front   Middle   Back

My Review:

Theme Park: _____   Date: _____

Location: _____   First Ride: Yes   No

Coaster Name: _____   Wait Time: _____

Park Area: _____   Ticket Price: _____

Weather: _____   Express Pass: Yes   No

Crowd: _____

Coaster Manufacturer: _____

Coaster Type: Wood   Steel   Hyper   Hybrid   Converted

Coaster Design: (circle all applicable options)

4th Dimension	Accelerator	Bobsled	Dive	Flying	Floorless
Inverted	Mine Train	Motorbike	Pipeline		Side Friction
Single Rail	Sit Down	Spinning	Stand Up	Suspended	Wing

Restraint Type:

Lap Bar	Lap Bar w/seatbelt	Shoulder Harness	Motorbike
Shoulder Harness w/seatbelt	Vest Harness	
Other:		

Coaster Stats

Height:	Number of Inversions:
Length:	Duration:
Speed:	Cars Per Train:
Drop:	Height Restrictions: min: max:

Other Restrictions: (i.e. lockers required, metal detector, etc.)

_____

My Rating: ☆ ☆ ☆ ☆ ☆   Seat Location: Front   Middle   Back

My Review:

_____

Theme Park: _____ Date: _____

Location: _____ First Ride: Yes   No

Coaster Name: _____ Wait Time: _____

Park Area: _____ Ticket Price: _____

Weather: _____ Express Pass: Yes   No

Crowd: _____

Coaster Manufacturer: _____

Coaster Type: Wood   Steel   Hyper   Hybrid   Converted

Coaster Design: (circle all applicable options)

4th Dimension	Accelerator	Bobsled	Dive	Flying	Floorless
Inverted	Mine Train	Motorbike	Pipeline		Side Friction
Single Rail	Sit Down	Spinning	Stand Up	Suspended	Wing

Restraint Type:

| Lap Bar   Lap Bar w/seatbelt   Shoulder Harness   Motorbike |
| Shoulder Harness w/seatbelt   Vest Harness |
| Other: |

Coaster Stats

Height:	Number of Inversions:
Length:	Duration:
Speed:	Cars Per Train:
Drop:	Height Restrictions: min: max:

Other Restrictions: (i.e. lockers required, metal detector, etc.)

| |

My Rating: ☆ ☆ ☆ ☆ ☆   Seat Location: Front   Middle   Back

My Review:

| |

Theme Park: _____   Date: _____

Location: _____   First Ride: Yes   No

Coaster Name: _____   Wait Time: _____

Park Area: _____   Ticket Price: _____

Weather: _____   Express Pass: Yes   No

Crowd: _____

Coaster Manufacturer: _____

Coaster Type: Wood   Steel   Hyper   Hybrid   Converted

Coaster Design: (circle all applicable options)

4th Dimension	Accelerator	Bobsled	Dive	Flying	Floorless
Inverted	Mine Train	Motorbike	Pipeline		Side Friction
Single Rail	Sit Down	Spinning	Stand Up	Suspended	Wing

Restraint Type:

Lap Bar   Lap Bar w/seatbelt   Shoulder Harness   Motorbike

Shoulder Harness w/seatbelt   Vest Harness

Other: _____

Coaster Stats

Height:	Number of Inversions:
Length:	Duration:
Speed:	Cars Per Train:
Drop:	Height Restrictions: min: max:

Other Restrictions: (i.e. lockers required, metal detector, etc.)

My Rating: ☆ ☆ ☆ ☆ ☆   Seat Location: Front   Middle   Back

My Review:

Theme Park: _____   Date: _____

Location: _____   First Ride: Yes   No

Coaster Name: _____   Wait Time: _____

Park Area: _____   Ticket Price: _____

Weather: _____   Express Pass: Yes   No

Crowd: _____

Coaster Manufacturer: _____

Coaster Type: Wood   Steel   Hyper   Hybrid   Converted

Coaster Design: (circle all applicable options)

4th Dimension	Accelerator	Bobsled	Dive	Flying	Floorless
Inverted	Mine Train	Motorbike	Pipeline		Side Friction
Single Rail	Sit Down	Spinning	Stand Up	Suspended	Wing

Restraint Type:

Lap Bar	Lap Bar w/seatbelt	Shoulder Harness	Motorbike
Shoulder Harness w/seatbelt	Vest Harness		
Other:			

Coaster Stats

Height:	Number of Inversions:
Length:	Duration:
Speed:	Cars Per Train:
Drop:	Height Restrictions: min: max:

Other Restrictions: (i.e. lockers required, metal detector, etc.)

My Rating: ☆ ☆ ☆ ☆ ☆   Seat Location: Front   Middle   Back

My Review:

Theme Park: _____   Date: _____

Location: _____   First Ride: Yes   No

Coaster Name: _____   Wait Time: _____

Park Area: _____   Ticket Price: _____

Weather: _____   Express Pass: Yes   No

Crowd: _____

Coaster Manufacturer: _____

Coaster Type: Wood   Steel   Hyper   Hybrid   Converted

Coaster Design: (circle all applicable options)

4th Dimension	Accelerator	Bobsled	Dive	Flying	Floorless
Inverted	Mine Train	Motorbike	Pipeline		Side Friction
Single Rail	Sit Down	Spinning	Stand Up	Suspended	Wing

Restraint Type:

Lap Bar   Lap Bar w/seatbelt   Shoulder Harness   Motorbike

Shoulder Harness w/seatbelt   Vest Harness

Other: _____

Coaster Stats

Height:	Number of Inversions:
Length:	Duration:
Speed:	Cars Per Train:
Drop:	Height Restrictions: min: max:

Other Restrictions: (i.e. lockers required, metal detector, etc.)

My Rating: ☆ ☆ ☆ ☆ ☆   Seat Location: Front   Middle   Back

My Review:

Theme Park: _____ Date: _____

Location: _____ First Ride: Yes   No

Coaster Name: _____ Wait Time: _____

Park Area: _____ Ticket Price: _____

Weather: _____ Express Pass: Yes   No

Crowd: _____

Coaster Manufacturer: _____

Coaster Type: Wood   Steel   Hyper   Hybrid   Converted

Coaster Design: (circle all applicable options)

4th Dimension	Accelerator	Bobsled	Dive	Flying	Floorless
Inverted	Mine Train	Motorbike	Pipeline		Side Friction
Single Rail	Sit Down	Spinning	Stand Up	Suspended	Wing

Restraint Type:

Lap Bar	Lap Bar w/seatbelt	Shoulder Harness	Motorbike
Shoulder Harness w/seatbelt	Vest Harness		
Other:			

Coaster Stats

Height:	Number of Inversions:
Length:	Duration:
Speed:	Cars Per Train:
Drop:	Height Restrictions: min: max:

Other Restrictions: (i.e. lockers required, metal detector, etc.)

My Rating: ☆ ☆ ☆ ☆ ☆   Seat Location: Front   Middle   Back

My Review:

Theme Park: _____ Date: _____

Location: _____ First Ride: Yes   No

Coaster Name: _____ Wait Time: _____

Park Area: _____ Ticket Price: _____

Weather: _____ Express Pass: Yes   No

Crowd: _____

Coaster Manufacturer: _____

Coaster Type: Wood   Steel   Hyper   Hybrid   Converted

Coaster Design: (circle all applicable options)

4th Dimension	Accelerator	Bobsled	Dive	Flying	Floorless
Inverted	Mine Train	Motorbike	Pipeline		Side Friction
Single Rail	Sit Down	Spinning	Stand Up	Suspended	Wing

Restraint Type:

Lap Bar   Lap Bar w/seatbelt   Shoulder Harness   Motorbike

Shoulder Harness w/seatbelt   Vest Harness

Other:

Coaster Stats

Height:	Number of Inversions:
Length:	Duration:
Speed:	Cars Per Train:
Drop:	Height Restrictions: min: max:

Other Restrictions: (i.e. lockers required, metal detector, etc.)

My Rating: ☆☆☆☆☆   Seat Location: Front   Middle   Back

My Review:

Theme Park: _____ Date: _____

Location: _____ First Ride: Yes   No

Coaster Name: _____ Wait Time: _____

Park Area: _____ Ticket Price: _____

Weather: _____ Express Pass: Yes   No

Crowd: _____

Coaster Manufacturer: _____

Coaster Type: Wood   Steel   Hyper   Hybrid   Converted

Coaster Design: (circle all applicable options)

4th Dimension	Accelerator	Bobsled	Dive	Flying	Floorless
Inverted	Mine Train	Motorbike		Pipeline	Side Friction
Single Rail	Sit Down	Spinning	Stand Up	Suspended	Wing

Restraint Type:

Lap Bar	Lap Bar w/seatbelt	Shoulder Harness Motorbike
Shoulder Harness w/seatbelt	Vest Harness	
Other:		

Coaster Stats

Height:	Number of Inversions:
Length:	Duration:
Speed:	Cars Per Train:
Drop:	Height Restrictions: min: max:

Other Restrictions: (i.e. lockers required, metal detector, etc.)

My Rating: ☆☆☆☆☆   Seat Location: Front   Middle   Back

My Review:

118

Theme Park: _____ Date: _____

Location: _____ First Ride: Yes No

Coaster Name: _____ Wait Time: _____

Park Area: _____ Ticket Price: _____

Weather: _____ Express Pass: Yes No

Crowd: _____

Coaster Manufacturer: _____

Coaster Type: Wood   Steel   Hyper   Hybrid   Converted

Coaster Design: (circle all applicable options)

4th Dimension	Accelerator	Bobsled	Dive	Flying	Floorless
Inverted	Mine Train	Motorbike	Pipeline		Side Friction
Single Rail	Sit Down	Spinning	Stand Up	Suspended	Wing

Restraint Type:

Lap Bar   Lap Bar w/seatbelt   Shoulder Harness   Motorbike

Shoulder Harness w/seatbelt   Vest Harness

Other: _____

Coaster Stats

Height:	Number of Inversions:
Length:	Duration:
Speed:	Cars Per Train:
Drop:	Height Restrictions: min: max:

Other Restrictions: (i.e. lockers required, metal detector, etc.)

My Rating: ☆☆☆☆☆   Seat Location: Front   Middle   Back

My Review:

119

Theme Park: _____ Date: _____

Location: _____ First Ride: Yes   No

Coaster Name: _____ Wait Time: _____

Park Area: _____ Ticket Price: _____

Weather: _____ Express Pass: Yes   No

Crowd: _____

Coaster Manufacturer: _____

Coaster Type: Wood   Steel   Hyper   Hybrid   Converted

Coaster Design: (circle all applicable options)

4th Dimension	Accelerator	Bobsled	Dive	Flying	Floorless
Inverted	Mine Train	Motorbike	Pipeline		Side Friction
Single Rail	Sit Down	Spinning	Stand Up	Suspended	Wing

Restraint Type:

Lap Bar   Lap Bar w/seatbelt   Shoulder Harness   Motorbike

Shoulder Harness w/seatbelt   Vest Harness

Other: _____

Coaster Stats

Height:	Number of Inversions:
Length:	Duration:
Speed:	Cars Per Train:
Drop:	Height Restrictions: min: max:

Other Restrictions: (i.e. lockers required, metal detector, etc.)

My Rating: ☆ ☆ ☆ ☆ ☆   Seat Location: Front   Middle   Back

My Review:

Theme Park: _____ | Date: _____

Location: _____ | First Ride: Yes   No

Coaster Name: _____ | Wait Time: _____

Park Area: _____ | Ticket Price: _____

Weather: _____ | Express Pass: Yes No

Crowd: _____

Coaster Manufacturer: _____

Coaster Type: Wood   Steel   Hyper   Hybrid   Converted

Coaster Design: (circle all applicable options)

4th Dimension	Accelerator	Bobsled	Dive	Flying	Floorless
Inverted	Mine Train	Motorbike	Pipeline		Side Friction
Single Rail	Sit Down	Spinning	Stand Up	Suspended	Wing

Restraint Type:

Lap Bar   Lap Bar w/seatbelt   Shoulder Harness   Motorbike

Shoulder Harness w/seatbelt   Vest Harness

Other:

Coaster Stats

Height:	Number of Inversions:
Length:	Duration:
Speed:	Cars Per Train:
Drop:	Height Restrictions: min: max:

Other Restrictions: (i.e. lockers required, metal detector, etc.)

My Rating: ☆ ☆ ☆ ☆ ☆   Seat Location: Front   Middle   Back

My Review:

Theme Park: _____ Date: _____

Location: _____ First Ride: Yes   No

Coaster Name: _____ Wait Time: _____

Park Area: _____ Ticket Price: _____

Weather: _____ Express Pass: Yes   No

Crowd: _____

Coaster Manufacturer: _____

Coaster Type: Wood   Steel   Hyper   Hybrid   Converted

Coaster Design: (circle all applicable options)

4th Dimension	Accelerator	Bobsled	Dive	Flying	Floorless
Inverted	Mine Train	Motorbike	Pipeline		Side Friction
Single Rail	Sit Down	Spinning	Stand Up	Suspended	Wing

Restraint Type:

Lap Bar   Lap Bar w/seatbelt   Shoulder Harness   Motorbike

Shoulder Harness w/seatbelt   Vest Harness

Other: _____

Coaster Stats

Height:	Number of Inversions:
Length:	Duration:
Speed:	Cars Per Train:
Drop:	Height Restrictions: min: max:

Other Restrictions: (i.e. lockers required, metal detector, etc.)

My Rating: ☆ ☆ ☆ ☆ ☆   Seat Location: Front   Middle   Back

My Review:

Theme Park: _____ Date: _____

Location: _____ First Ride: Yes   No

Coaster Name: _____ Wait Time: _____

Park Area: _____ Ticket Price: _____

Weather: _____ Express Pass: Yes   No

Crowd: _____

Coaster Manufacturer: _____

Coaster Type: Wood   Steel   Hyper   Hybrid   Converted

Coaster Design: (circle all applicable options)

4th Dimension	Accelerator	Bobsled	Dive	Flying	Floorless
Inverted	Mine Train	Motorbike	Pipeline		Side Friction
Single Rail	Sit Down	Spinning	Stand Up	Suspended	Wing

Restraint Type:

Lap Bar	Lap Bar w/seatbelt	Shoulder Harness	Motorbike
Shoulder Harness w/seatbelt	Vest Harness	
Other:		

Coaster Stats

Height:	Number of Inversions:
Length:	Duration:
Speed:	Cars Per Train:
Drop:	Height Restrictions: min: max:

Other Restrictions: (i.e. lockers required, metal detector, etc.)

_____

My Rating: ☆ ☆ ☆ ☆ ☆   Seat Location: Front   Middle   Back

My Review:

_____

Theme Park: _____   Date: _____

Location: _____   First Ride: Yes   No

Coaster Name: _____   Wait Time: _____

Park Area: _____   Ticket Price: _____

Weather: _____   Express Pass: Yes No

Crowd: _____

Coaster Manufacturer: _____

Coaster Type: Wood   Steel   Hyper   Hybrid   Converted

Coaster Design: (circle all applicable options)

4th Dimension	Accelerator	Bobsled	Dive	Flying	Floorless
Inverted	Mine Train	Motorbike		Pipeline	Side Friction
Single Rail	Sit Down	Spinning	Stand Up	Suspended	Wing

Restraint Type:

Lap Bar   Lap Bar w/seatbelt   Shoulder Harness   Motorbike

Shoulder Harness w/seatbelt   Vest Harness

Other: _____

Coaster Stats

Height:	Number of Inversions:
Length:	Duration:
Speed:	Cars Per Train:
Drop:	Height Restrictions: min: max:

Other Restrictions: (i.e. lockers required, metal detector, etc.)

My Rating: ☆ ☆ ☆ ☆ ☆   Seat Location: Front   Middle   Back

My Review:

Theme Park: _____ Date: _____

Location: _____ First Ride: Yes   No

Coaster Name: _____ Wait Time: _____

Park Area: _____ Ticket Price: _____

Weather: _____ Express Pass: Yes   No

Crowd: _____

Coaster Manufacturer: _____

Coaster Type: Wood   Steel   Hyper   Hybrid   Converted

Coaster Design: (circle all applicable options)

4th Dimension   Accelerator   Bobsled   Dive   Flying   Floorless

Inverted   Mine Train   Motorbike   Pipeline   Side Friction

Single Rail   Sit Down   Spinning   Stand Up   Suspended   Wing

Restraint Type:

Lap Bar   Lap Bar w/seatbelt   Shoulder Harness   Motorbike

Shoulder Harness w/seatbelt   Vest Harness

Other:

Coaster Stats

Height:	Number of Inversions:
Length:	Duration:
Speed:	Cars Per Train:
Drop:	Height Restrictions: min: max:

Other Restrictions: (i.e. lockers required, metal detector, etc.)

My Rating: ☆ ☆ ☆ ☆ ☆   Seat Location: Front   Middle   Back

My Review:

Theme Park: _____ Date: _____

Location: _____

Coaster Name: _____

Park Area: _____

Weather: _____

Crowd: _____

Coaster Manufacturer: _____

Coaster Type: Wood   Steel   Hyper   ...

4th Dimension   Accelerator   Bobsled   Dive   Flying   Floorless

Inverted   Mine Train   Motorbike   Pipeline   Side Friction

Single Rail   Sit Down   Spinning   Stand Up   Suspended   Wing

Restraint Type:

Lap Bar   Lap Bar w/seatbelt   Shoulder Harness   Motorbike

Shoulder Harness w/seatbelt   Vest Harness

Other: _____

Height: _____

Length: _____

Speed: _____   Cars Per Train: _____

Drop: _____   Height Restrictions: min: _____ max: _____

Other Restrictions: (i.e. lockers required, metal detector, etc.)

My Rating: ☆ ☆ ☆ ☆ ☆   Seat Location: Front   Middle   Back

My Review:

Theme Park: _____ Date: _____

Location: _____ First Ride: Yes   No

Coaster Name: _____ Wait Time: _____

Park Area: _____ Ticket Price: _____

Weather: _____ Express Pass: Yes   No

Crowd: _____

Coaster Manufacturer: _____

Coaster Type: Wood   Steel   Hyper   Hybrid   Converted

Coaster Design: (circle all applicable options)

4th Dimension	Accelerator	Bobsled	Dive	Flying	Floorless
Inverted	Mine Train	Motorbike	Pipeline		Side Friction
Single Rail	Sit Down	Spinning	Stand Up	Suspended	Wing

Restraint Type:

Lap Bar	Lap Bar w/seatbelt	Shoulder Harness	Motorbike
Shoulder Harness w/seatbelt		Vest Harness	
Other:			

Coaster Stats

Height:	Number of Inversions:
Length:	Duration:
Speed:	Cars Per Train:
Drop:	Height Restrictions: min: max:

Other Restrictions: (i.e. lockers required, metal detector, etc.)

My Rating: ☆☆☆☆☆   Seat Location: Front   Middle   Back

My Review:

Theme Park: _____   Date: _____

Location: _____   First Ride: Yes No

Coaster Name: _____   Wait Time: _____

Park Area: _____   Ticket Price: _____

Weather: _____   Express Pass: Yes No

Crowd: _____

Coaster Manufacturer: _____

Coaster Type: Wood   Steel   Hyper   Hybrid   Converted

Coaster Design: (circle all applicable options)

4th Dimension	Accelerator	Bobsled	Dive	Flying	Floorless
Inverted	Mine Train	Motorbike	Pipeline		Side Friction
Single Rail	Sit Down	Spinning	Stand Up	Suspended	Wing

Restraint Type:

Lap Bar   Lap Bar w/seatbelt   Shoulder Harness   Motorbike

Shoulder Harness w/seatbelt   Vest Harness

Other:

Coaster Stats

Height:	Number of Inversions:
Length:	Duration:
Speed:	Cars Per Train:
Drop:	Height Restrictions: min: max:

Other Restrictions: (i.e. lockers required, metal detector, etc.)

My Rating: ☆☆☆☆☆   Seat Location: Front   Middle   Back

My Review:

Theme Park: _____   Date: _____

Location: _____   First Ride: Yes   No

Coaster Name: _____   Wait Time: _____

Park Area: _____   Ticket Price: _____

Weather: _____   Express Pass: Yes   No

Crowd: _____

Coaster Manufacturer: _____

Coaster Type: Wood   Steel   Hyper   Hybrid   Converted

Coaster Design: (circle all applicable options)

4th Dimension	Accelerator	Bobsled	Dive	Flying	Floorless
Inverted	Mine Train	Motorbike	Pipeline		Side Friction
Single Rail	Sit Down	Spinning	Stand Up	Suspended	Wing

Restraint Type:

Lap Bar Lap Bar w/seatbelt Shoulder Harness Motorbike	
Shoulder Harness w/seatbelt Vest Harness	
Other:	

Coaster Stats

Height:	Number of Inversions:
Length:	Duration:
Speed:	Cars Per Train:
Drop:	Height Restrictions: min: max:

Other Restrictions: (i.e. lockers required, metal detector, etc.)

My Rating: ☆ ☆ ☆ ☆ ☆   Seat Location: Front   Middle   Back

My Review:

Theme Park: _____ Date: _____

Location: _____ First Ride: Yes   No

Coaster Name: _____ Wait Time: _____

Park Area: _____ Ticket Price: _____

Weather: _____ Express Pass: Yes   No

Crowd: _____

Coaster Manufacturer: _____

Coaster Type: Wood   Steel   Hyper   Hybrid   Converted

Coaster Design: (circle all applicable options)

4th Dimension	Accelerator	Bobsled	Dive	Flying	Floorless
Inverted	Mine Train	Motorbike		Pipeline	Side Friction
Single Rail	Sit Down	Spinning	Stand Up	Suspended	Wing

Restraint Type:

Lap Bar   Lap Bar w/seatbelt   Shoulder Harness   Motorbike

Shoulder Harness w/seatbelt   Vest Harness

Other: _____

Coaster Stats

Height:	Number of Inversions:
Length:	Duration:
Speed:	Cars Per Train:
Drop:	Height Restrictions: min: max:

Other Restrictions: (i.e. lockers required, metal detector, etc.)

My Rating: ☆ ☆ ☆ ☆ ☆   Seat Location: Front   Middle   Back

My Review:

Theme Park: _____   Date: _____

Location: _____   First Ride: Yes   No

Coaster Name: _____   Wait Time: _____

Park Area: _____   Ticket Price: _____

Weather: _____   Express Pass: Yes   No

Crowd: _____

Coaster Manufacturer: _____

Coaster Type: Wood   Steel   Hyper   Hybrid   Converted

Coaster Design: (circle all applicable options)

4th Dimension	Accelerator	Bobsled	Dive	Flying	Floorless
Inverted	Mine Train	Motorbike	Pipeline		Side Friction
Single Rail	Sit Down	Spinning	Stand Up	Suspended	Wing

Restraint Type:

Lap Bar   Lap Bar w/seatbelt   Shoulder Harness   Motorbike

Shoulder Harness w/seatbelt   Vest Harness

Other:

Coaster Stats

Height:	Number of Inversions:
Length:	Duration:
Speed:	Cars Per Train:
Drop:	Height Restrictions: min: max:

Other Restrictions: (i.e. lockers required, metal detector, etc.)

My Rating: ☆ ☆ ☆ ☆ ☆   Seat Location: Front   Middle   Back

My Review:

Theme Park: _____ Date: _____

Location: _____ First Ride: Yes No

Coaster Name: _____ Wait Time: _____

Park Area: _____ Ticket Price: _____

Weather: _____ Express Pass: Yes No

Crowd: _____

Coaster Manufacturer: _____

Coaster Type: Wood   Steel   Hyper   Hybrid   Converted

Coaster Design: (circle all applicable options)

4th Dimension	Accelerator	Bobsled	Dive	Flying	Floorless
Inverted	Mine Train	Motorbike	Pipeline		Side Friction
Single Rail	Sit Down	Spinning	Stand Up	Suspended	Wing

Restraint Type:

Lap Bar   Lap Bar w/seatbelt   Shoulder Harness   Motorbike

Shoulder Harness w/seatbelt   Vest Harness

Other:

Coaster Stats

Height:	Number of Inversions:
Length:	Duration:
Speed:	Cars Per Train:
Drop:	Height Restrictions: min: max:

Other Restrictions: (i.e. lockers required, metal detector, etc.)

My Rating: ☆ ☆ ☆ ☆ ☆   Seat Location: Front Middle Back

My Review:

Theme Park: _____ Date: _____

Location: _____ First Ride: Yes   No

Coaster Name: _____ Wait Time: _____

Park Area: _____ Ticket Price: _____

Weather: _____ Express Pass: Yes   No

Crowd: _____

Coaster Manufacturer: _____

Coaster Type: Wood   Steel   Hyper   Hybrid   Converted

Coaster Design: (circle all applicable options)

4th Dimension	Accelerator	Bobsled	Dive	Flying	Floorless
Inverted	Mine Train	Motorbike	Pipeline		Side Friction
Single Rail	Sit Down	Spinning	Stand Up	Suspended	Wing

Restraint Type:

Lap Bar   Lap Bar w/seatbelt   Shoulder Harness   Motorbike

Shoulder Harness w/seatbelt   Vest Harness

Other: _____

Coaster Stats

Height:	Number of Inversions:
Length:	Duration:
Speed:	Cars Per Train:
Drop:	Height Restrictions: min: max:

Other Restrictions: (i.e. lockers required, metal detector, etc.)

My Rating: ☆ ☆ ☆ ☆ ☆   Seat Location: Front   Middle   Back

My Review:

Theme Park: _____   Date: _____

Location: _____   First Ride: Yes   No

Coaster Name: _____   Wait Time: _____

Park Area: _____   Ticket Price: _____

Weather: _____   Express Pass: Yes   No

Crowd: _____

Coaster Manufacturer: _____

Coaster Type: Wood   Steel   Hyper   Hybrid   Converted

Coaster Design: (circle all applicable options)

4th Dimension	Accelerator	Bobsled	Dive	Flying	Floorless
Inverted	Mine Train	Motorbike	Pipeline		Side Friction
Single Rail	Sit Down	Spinning	Stand Up	Suspended	Wing

Restraint Type:

Lap Bar	Lap Bar w/seatbelt	Shoulder Harness	Motorbike
Shoulder Harness w/seatbelt		Vest Harness	
Other:			

Coaster Stats

Height:	Number of Inversions:
Length:	Duration:
Speed:	Cars Per Train:
Drop:	Height Restrictions: min: max:

Other Restrictions: (i.e. lockers required, metal detector, etc.)

My Rating: ☆ ☆ ☆ ☆ ☆   Seat Location: Front   Middle   Back

My Review:

Theme Park: _____ Date: _____

Location: _____ First Ride: Yes   No

Coaster Name: _____ Wait Time: _____

Park Area: _____ Ticket Price: _____

Weather: _____ Express Pass: Yes   No

Crowd: _____

Coaster Manufacturer: _____

Coaster Type: Wood   Steel   Hyper   Hybrid   Converted

Coaster Design: (circle all applicable options)

4th Dimension	Accelerator	Bobsled	Dive	Flying	Floorless
Inverted	Mine Train	Motorbike	Pipeline		Side Friction
Single Rail	Sit Down	Spinning	Stand Up	Suspended	Wing

Restraint Type:

Lap Bar	Lap Bar w/seatbelt	Shoulder Harness	Motorbike
Shoulder Harness w/seatbelt		Vest Harness	
Other:			

Coaster Stats

Height:	Number of Inversions:
Length:	Duration:
Speed:	Cars Per Train:
Drop:	Height Restrictions: min: max:

Other Restrictions: (i.e. lockers required, metal detector, etc.)

My Rating: ☆ ☆ ☆ ☆ ☆   Seat Location: Front   Middle   Back

My Review:

Theme Park: _____ Date: _____

Location: _____ First Ride: Yes No

Coaster Name: _____ Wait Time: _____

Park Area: _____ Ticket Price: _____

Weather: _____ Express Pass: Yes No

Crowd: _____

Coaster Manufacturer: _____

Coaster Type: Wood Steel Hyper Hybrid Converted

Coaster Design: (circle all applicable options)

4th Dimension	Accelerator	Bobsled	Dive	Flying	Floorless
Inverted	Mine Train	Motorbike	Pipeline		Side Friction
Single Rail	Sit Down	Spinning	Stand Up	Suspended	Wing

Restraint Type:

Lap Bar	Lap Bar w/seatbelt	Shoulder Harness	Motorbike
Shoulder Harness w/seatbelt	Vest Harness	
Other:		

Coaster Stats

Height:	Number of Inversions:
Length:	Duration:
Speed:	Cars Per Train:
Drop:	Height Restrictions: min: max:

Other Restrictions: (i.e. lockers required, metal detector, etc.)

My Rating: ☆ ☆ ☆ ☆ ☆   Seat Location: Front Middle Back

My Review:

Theme Park: _____ Date: _____

Location: _____ First Ride: Yes   No

Coaster Name: _____ Wait Time: _____

Park Area: _____ Ticket Price: _____

Weather: _____ Express Pass: Yes No

Crowd: _____

Coaster Manufacturer: _____

Coaster Type: Wood   Steel   Hyper   Hybrid   Converted

Coaster Design: (circle all applicable options)

4th Dimension	Accelerator	Bobsled	Dive	Flying	Floorless
Inverted	Mine Train	Motorbike	Pipeline		Side Friction
Single Rail	Sit Down	Spinning	Stand Up	Suspended	Wing

Restraint Type:

Lap Bar   Lap Bar w/seatbelt   Shoulder Harness   Motorbike

Shoulder Harness w/seatbelt   Vest Harness

Other:

Coaster Stats

Height:	Number of Inversions:
Length:	Duration:
Speed:	Cars Per Train:
Drop:	Height Restrictions: min: max:

Other Restrictions: (i.e. lockers required, metal detector, etc.)

My Rating: ☆☆☆☆☆   Seat Location: Front   Middle   Back

My Review:

Theme Park: _____   Date: _____

Location: _____   First Ride: Yes   No

Coaster Name: _____   Wait Time: _____

Park Area: _____   Ticket Price: _____

Weather: _____   Express Pass: Yes   No

Crowd: _____

Coaster Manufacturer: _____

Coaster Type: Wood   Steel   Hyper   Hybrid   Converted

Coaster Design: (circle all applicable options)

4th Dimension	Accelerator	Bobsled	Dive	Flying	Floorless
Inverted	Mine Train	Motorbike	Pipeline		Side Friction
Single Rail	Sit Down	Spinning	Stand Up	Suspended	Wing

Restraint Type:

Lap Bar   Lap Bar w/seatbelt   Shoulder Harness   Motorbike

Shoulder Harness w/seatbelt   Vest Harness

Other:

Coaster Stats

Height:	Number of Inversions:
Length:	Duration:
Speed:	Cars Per Train:
Drop:	Height Restrictions: min: max:

Other Restrictions: (i.e. lockers required, metal detector, etc.)

My Rating: ☆ ☆ ☆ ☆ ☆   Seat Location: Front   Middle   Back

My Review:

Theme Park: _____ Date: _____

Location: _____ First Ride: Yes   No

Coaster Name: _____ Wait Time: _____

Park Area: _____ Ticket Price: _____

Weather: _____ Express Pass: Yes No

Crowd: _____

Coaster Manufacturer: _____

Coaster Type: Wood   Steel   Hyper   Hybrid   Converted

Coaster Design: (circle all applicable options)

4th Dimension	Accelerator	Bobsled	Dive	Flying	Floorless
Inverted	Mine Train	Motorbike	Pipeline		Side Friction
Single Rail	Sit Down	Spinning	Stand Up	Suspended	Wing

Restraint Type:

Lap Bar   Lap Bar w/seatbelt   Shoulder Harness   Motorbike

Shoulder Harness w/seatbelt   Vest Harness

Other:

Coaster Stats

Height:	Number of Inversions:
Length:	Duration:
Speed:	Cars Per Train:
Drop:	Height Restrictions: min: max:

Other Restrictions: (i.e. lockers required, metal detector, etc.)

My Rating: ☆☆☆☆☆   Seat Location: Front   Middle   Back

My Review:

Theme Park: _____ Date: _____

Location: _____ First Ride: Yes   No

Coaster Name: _____ Wait Time: _____

Park Area: _____ Ticket Price: _____

Weather: _____ Express Pass: Yes   No

Crowd: _____

Coaster Manufacturer: _____

Coaster Type: Wood   Steel   Hyper   Hybrid   Converted

Coaster Design: (circle all applicable options)

4th Dimension	Accelerator	Bobsled	Dive	Flying	Floorless
Inverted	Mine Train	Motorbike		Pipeline	Side Friction
Single Rail	Sit Down	Spinning	Stand Up	Suspended	Wing

Restraint Type:

Lap Bar	Lap Bar w/seatbelt	Shoulder Harness	Motorbike
Shoulder Harness w/seatbelt		Vest Harness	
Other:			

Coaster Stats

Height:	Number of Inversions:
Length:	Duration:
Speed:	Cars Per Train:
Drop:	Height Restrictions: min: max:

Other Restrictions: (i.e. lockers required, metal detector, etc.)

_____

My Rating: ☆ ☆ ☆ ☆ ☆   Seat Location: Front   Middle   Back

My Review:

_____

Printed in Great Britain
by Amazon